MW00780343

Theotókos
Woman, Mother, Disciple
A Catechesis on Mary, Mother of God

Pope John Paul II

With a Foreword by
Eamon R. Carroll, O.Carm., S.T.D.

BOOKS & MEDIA

BOSTON

Library of Congress Cataloging-in-Publication Data

John Paul II, Pope, 1920–
    Theotókos : Mary, Mother of God / John Paul II ; with
foreword by Eamon R. Carroll.
        p.   cm.
    "This volume comprises seventy general audience talks on
Mary which were delivered from September 1995 to November 1997"—Foreword.
    Includes bibliographical references and index.
    ISBN 0-8198-7401-9 (pbk.)
    1. Mary, Blessed Virgin, Saint—Theology.   2. Catholic
Church—Doctrines.   I. Title.
BT613.J63   1998
232.91—dc21   98–46201
                                                     CIP

Reprinted with permission from *L'Osservatore Romano,* English
Edition.

Cover: *Icona Russa: Madonna di Kazan*

Printed and published in the U.S.A. by Pauline Books & Media,
50 Saint Pauls Avenue, Boston MA 02130-3491.

www.pauline.org

Pauline Books & Media is the publishing house of the Daughters
of St. Paul, an international congregation of women religious
serving the Church with the communications media.

    2 3 4 5 6   05 04 03 02 01

The following abbreviations are used in the text
to indicate certain documents:

CCC   *Catechism of the Catholic Church*

DS   *Denzinger-Schönmetzer*

LG   *Lumen Gentium* (Dogmatic Constitution on the
       Church)

MC   *Marialis Cultus* (For the Right Ordering and
       Development of Devotion to the Blessed Virgin
       Mary)

RM   *Redemptoris Mater* (Mother of the Redeemer)

SC   *Sacrosanctum Concilium* (Constitution on the
       Sacred Liturgy)

Contents

Foreword

John Paul II will be remembered for so many great things that even a short inventory would take pages. In his pontificate, so strongly marked by a Marian character, the Holy Father has given significant teachings about our Blessed Mother. This volume comprises seventy general audience talks on Mary which were delivered from September 1995 to November 1997.

Like the scribe Our Lord spoke of who brings forth from his storehouse things new and old (cf. Mt 13:52), the Pope explores the richness of the Church's Marian heritage in a contemporary way. His series of instructions about our Blessed Lady form an easy-to-follow course in Marian doctrine and devotion—the theology of the holy Mother of God, what the Church believes about her, and how we are to respond to her as our spiritual Mother. Pope John Paul II is a master teacher. Reaching back into the Scriptures and early Christian authors, the Holy Father also reports on subsequent developments in teaching and practice about the Blessed Virgin. He explains all the Church's teachings about Mary—her role as Mother of God, ever-virgin, graced with total holiness from her immaculate conception, her free and faithful cooperation in God's saving plan, her assumption, her mediatorial role as derived from that of Christ, our "one mediator" (1 Tm 2:5–6), and her role as our loving spiritual mother.

The Second Vatican Council, which the Holy Father attended as Bishop Karol Wojtyla, stated with marvelous clarity in its first document that "Blessed Mary, Mother of God...is joined by an inseparable bond to the saving work of her Son" (*SC* 103), so that in celebrating the yearly cycle of the mysteries of Christ the Church honors the Blessed Virgin with special love. "In her the Church holds up and admires the most excellent fruit of the redemption, and joyfully contemplates, as in a faultless image, that which the Church herself wholly desires and hopes wholly to be" (*SC* 103). A year later, the Council issued the *Dogmatic Constitution on the Church* (November 21, 1964), with its concluding chapter on "The Blessed Virgin Mary, Mother of God, in the Mystery of Christ and the Church."

On February 2, 1974, Pope Paul VI gave the Church *Marialis Cultus,* his letter on devotion to Mary, especially in the liturgy. Pope John Paul weaves all these rich Marian materials into the catechetical homilies in this collection, including other statements of his own. In particular he draws on the encyclical *Mother of the Redeemer,* which he issued on the feast of the Annunciation, March 25, 1987, for the Marian Year which extended from Pentecost (June 7, 1987) to the feast of our Lady's Assumption (August 15, 1988). As this volume illustrates, the Holy Father has reviewed the principal teachings of his pontificate in the light of our Lady. The Mother of Jesus has served him as the prism through which to examine his major monumental messages to the Church and to the world, concerning the gift of life, the rights of women, the dignity of work, the goal of peace and the desire for Christian unity.

This wide spectrum of teaching is evident from the first talk, MARY IS A PATTERN OF THE CHURCH'S HOLINESS to the final one, OUR SEPARATED BRETHREN ALSO HONOR MARY. Here are some thoughts from the series that struck me, offered in the realization that each reader will choose from this treasure-trove items suited to individual taste.

The co-presence of the gifts of virginity and maternity in the maiden of Nazareth has led Christians to call Mary simply "the Virgin," even when they celebrate her divine motherhood (9/13/95). In all Mary's shrines, the memory of events associated with her intercession conveys the message of her motherly tenderness, opening our hearts to God's grace. The Holy Spirit has spurred Christian faith to discover Mary's face (11/15/95). Mary is a model of persevering silence—her serenity of spirit gives the Church a joyful face (1/3/96). The pope notes that "Mary's place is the highest after Christ." Accordingly, "the entire teaching of salvation history invites us to look to the Virgin…that we might welcome her as children in faith" (1/3/96).

In the talk titled THE BLESSED VIRGIN WAS FILLED WITH GOD'S GRACE, one of several such homilies, we find "*Full of grace* is the name Mary possesses in the eyes of God…not merely *full of grace,* but *made full of grace,* or even *filled with grace,* which would clearly indicate that this was a gift God gave to the Blessed Virgin" (5/8/96). On several occasions the pope describes Mary as the new Eve, evoking the contrast between the disobedience of the first Eve and the salutary obedience of the Blessed Virgin. Following the lead of the *Catechism of the Catholic Church,* he quotes St. Irenaeus (d. about 203): "being obedient, she became the cause of salvation for herself and for the whole human race" (9/18/96).

The Gospel mysteries recalled in the rosary receive careful attention, as in the talk titled THE VISITATION IS A PRELUDE TO JESUS' MISSION (10/2/96). In the Hail Mary, believers echo the exclamation of Elizabeth "as the Church's song of praise for the great works the Most High accomplished in the Mother of his Son." At the birth of Jesus "the Mother of God joyfully showed her firstborn Son" to the visiting shepherds. "It was the defining moment of their lives" (11/20/96). In discussing the presentation in the temple, the Pope notes that Simeon's prophecy is "almost a 'second annunciation' which will lead the Virgin to a deeper understanding of her Son's destiny" (12/18/ 96; cf. also *RM* 16).

The next address, CHRIST CALLS WOMEN TO SHARE HIS MISSION continues the reflection on the presentation. Anna is "a symbol of the women who, dedicated to spreading the Gospel, will arouse and nourish the hope of salvation" (1/8/97).

The pope also draws a series of lessons from the wedding feast of Cana (2/26/97; 3/5/97). Mary strengthened the faith of the disciples by obtaining the miracle; she showed us what a mother's love can do. John Paul quotes Vatican II's description of Mary at Cana as "moved with pity"; "letting it be understood that Mary was prompted by her merciful heart." This reminded me of the American poet John Ciardi's reflection on Dante's reference to Cana in his *Divine Comedy*—of Mary's "gentle dismay" at the failing wedding wine.

In the talk MARY HAD A ROLE IN JESUS' PUBLIC MINISTRY (3/ 12/97), where the Pope comments on the fact that Mary did not follow her Son in his public ministry, we find the lovely line: "Separation did not mean distance of heart, nor did it prevent the Mother from spiritually following her Son, from keeping and meditating on his teaching as she had done during Jesus' hidden life in Nazareth." In the meditation on Mary as a model of the Church at prayer, John Paul states that Mary encourages "the faithful to desire an intimate, personal relationship with Christ in order to cooperate with the gift of their own lives in the salvation of all" (9/10/97). He then goes on to explain the meaning of Mary's title as "Mother of the Church," which Paul VI had proclaimed during the Council.

The final talks discuss devotion to Mary, as the Church has always practiced it: "Since the Church's earliest days, Marian devotion has been meant to foster faithful adherence to Christ"

(10/22/97). "As the liturgy and Christian piety demonstrate, the Church has always held devotion to Mary in high esteem, considering it inseparably linked to belief in Christ. It is based on the Father's plan, the Savior's will and the Paraclete's inspiration" (11/5/97).

The last talk, which deals with ecumenism, is filled with hope: "Catholics have a deep desire to be able to share with all their brothers and sisters in Christ the joy that comes from Mary's presence in life according to the Spirit" (11/12/97). It is fitting that this series of catechetical instructions about the Blessed Virgin, holy Mother of God, and our loving spiritual mother, should close with the Holy Father's "cry from the heart" for Christian unity. He has voiced this theme and prayer so often, especially in his encyclical on ecumenism, *Ut Unum Sint.* It is his fervent desire that through Mary's intercession, full communion among all believers in Christ may finally be attained.

Rev. Eamon R. Carroll, O.Carm., S.T.D.

Professor emeritus of theology,
Loyola University of Chicago

On the staff of IMRI
(the International Marian Research Institute),
Marian Library, University of Dayton, Ohio.

Mary Is a Pattern of the Church's Holiness

After pausing in the previous catecheses to reflect more deeply on the identity and mission of the Church, I now feel the need to turn our gaze to the Blessed Virgin. She is the perfect realization of the Church's holiness and its model.

This is exactly what the Fathers of the Second Vatican Council did. After explaining the doctrine on the reality of the People of God in salvation history, they wanted to complete it with an illustration of Mary's role in the work of salvation. The purpose of chapter eight of *Lumen Gentium* is to emphasize the ecclesiological significance of Marian doctrine, and likewise to shed light on the contribution that the figure of the Blessed Virgin offers to our understanding of the Church's mystery.

Before explaining the Council's Marian itinerary, I would like to take a reflective look at Mary just as, at the Church's beginning, she is described in the Acts of the Apostles. At the beginning of this New Testament text, which describes the life of the first Christian community, and after recording the names of the apostles one by one (1:13), Luke states: "All these with one accord devoted themselves to prayer, together with the women and Mary, the mother of Jesus, and with his brethren" (1:14).

The person of Mary stands out clearly in this picture. With the apostles, she is the only one mentioned by name. She represents one face of the Church, different from and complementary to the ministerial or hierarchical aspect.

Luke's statement mentions the presence in the upper room of some women, thus showing the importance of the feminine contribution to the Church's life from the very beginning. This presence is closely linked to the perseverance of the community in prayer and harmony. These traits perfectly express two basic aspects of women's specific contribution to ecclesial life. Better suited to outward activity, men need women's help to be brought back into personal relationships in order to progress toward the union of hearts.

"Blessed among women" (Lk 1:42), Mary eminently fulfills this feminine mission. Who better than Mary can encourage all believers to persevere in prayer? Who better than she can promote harmony and love?

Recognizing the pastoral mission Jesus entrusted to the eleven, the women in the upper room, with Mary in their midst, joined in their prayer. At the same time they witnessed to the presence in the Church of people who, although they have not received that mission, are likewise full-fledged members of the community gathered in faith in Christ.

Mary's presence in the community, which was waiting in prayer for the outpouring of the Spirit (cf. Acts 1:14), calls to mind her part in the Incarnation of the Son of God by the work of the Holy Spirit (cf. Lk 1:35). The Virgin's role in that initial stage and the role she played in the manifestation of the Church at Pentecost are closely linked.

Mary's presence at the first moments of the Church's life is remarkably highlighted by comparison with her previous, very discreet participation during Jesus' public ministry. When the Son began his mission, Mary remained in Nazareth, even though this separation did not exclude significant contacts such as the one at Cana. Above all, it did not prevent her from taking part in the sacrifice of Calvary. In the first community, however, Mary's role assumed notable importance. After the ascension and in expectation of Pentecost, Jesus' Mother was personally present at the first stages of the work begun by her Son.

The Acts of the Apostles stresses that Mary was in the upper room "with his [Jesus'] brethren" (Acts 1:14), that is, with his relatives, as has always been the Church's interpretation. It was not so much a family gathering as the fact that under Mary's guidance, Jesus' natural family came to be part of Christ's spiritual family: "Whoever does the will of God," Jesus had said, "is my brother and sister and mother" (Mk 3:35).

On the same occasion, Luke explicitly described Mary as "Mother of Jesus" (Acts 1:14), almost as if he wished to suggest that something of the presence of the Son who had ascended into heaven has remained in the presence of the mother. She reminded his disciples of Jesus' face, and with her presence in the community she was the symbol of the Church's fidelity to Christ the Lord.

In this context, the title "Mother" proclaims the attitude of thoughtful closeness with which our Lady followed the Church's life. Mary was to open her heart to the Church to show the marvels done in her by the almighty and merciful God.

From the beginning, Mary carried out her role as "Mother of the Church." Her action encouraged understanding among the apostles, whom Luke describes as being of "one accord," far from the disputes that had occasionally arisen among them.

Lastly, Mary expressed her motherhood toward the community of believers not only by praying to obtain for the Church the gifts of the Holy Spirit necessary for her formation and her future, but also by teaching the Lord's disciples about constant communion with God. Mary thus became the Christian people's teacher of prayer, of encounter with God, a central indispensable element, so that the work of the pastors and the faithful would always have its beginning and its inner motivation in the Lord.

From these brief remarks it can clearly be seen how the relationship between Mary and the Church is a fascinating comparison between two mothers. It clearly reveals Mary's maternal mission and the Church's commitment ever to seek her true identity in contemplation of the face of the *Theotókos*.

General audience of September 6, 1995

Mary Is the Virgin Mother of God

In *Lumen Gentium,* the Council stated that "joined to Christ the head and in the unity of fellowship with all his saints, the faithful must in the first place reverence the memory 'of the glorious ever-virgin Mary, Mother of our God and Lord Jesus Christ'" (n. 52). The conciliar Constitution uses these terms from the Roman Canon of the Mass, thereby stressing how faith in the divine motherhood of Mary has been present in Christian thought since the first centuries.

In the newborn Church, Mary is remembered with the title "Mother of Jesus." Luke himself gives her this title in the Acts of the Apostles, a title that corresponds to what the Gospels say: "Is this not...the son of Mary?" Thus the residents of Nazareth wonder according to the Evangelist Mark's account (6:3). "Isn't Mary known to be his mother?" is the question recorded by Matthew (13:55).

In the disciples' eyes, as they gathered after the ascension, the title "Mother of Jesus" acquired its full meaning. For them, Mary was a person unique in her kind: she received the singular grace of giving birth to the Savior of humanity; she lived for a long while at his side; and on Calvary she was called by the crucified one to exercise a "new motherhood" in relation to the beloved disciple and through him to the whole Church.

For those who believe in Jesus and follow him, "Mother of Jesus" is a title of honor and veneration, and will forever remain such in the faith and life of the Church. In a particular way, by this title Christians mean to say that one cannot refer to Jesus' origins without acknowledging the role of the woman who gave him birth in the Spirit according to his human nature. Her maternal role also involves the birth and growth of the Church. In recalling the place of Mary in Jesus' life, the faithful discover each day her efficacious presence in their own spiritual journey.

From the beginning, the Church has acknowledged the virginal motherhood of Mary. As the infancy Gospels enable us to grasp, the first Christian communities themselves gathered together Mary's recollections about the mysterious circumstances of the Savior's conception and birth. In particular, the annunciation account responds to the disciples' desire to have the deepest knowledge of the events connected with the beginnings of the risen Christ's earthly life. In the last analysis, Mary is at the origin of the revelation about the mystery of the virginal conception by the work of the Holy Spirit.

The first Christians immediately grasped the important significance of this truth showing Jesus' divine origin, and included it among the key affirmations of their faith. Son of Joseph according to the law, by an extraordinary intervention of the Holy Spirit Jesus was in his humanity only the son of Mary, since he was born without the intervention of man. Mary's virginity thus acquires a unique value and casts new light on the birth of Jesus and on the mystery of his sonship, since the virginal generation is the sign that Jesus has God himself as his Father.

Acknowledged and proclaimed by the faith of the Fathers, the virginal motherhood can never be separated from the identity of Jesus, true God and true man, as "born of the Virgin Mary," as we profess in the Nicene-Constantinopolitan Creed.

Mary is the only virgin who is also a mother. The extraordinary co-presence of these two gifts in the person of the maiden of Nazareth has led Christians to call Mary simply "the Virgin," even when they celebrate her motherhood.

The virginity of Mary thus initiates in the Christian community the spread of the virginal life, embraced by all who are called to it by the Lord. This special vocation, which reaches its apex in Christ's example, represents immeasurable spiritual wealth for the Church in every age, which finds in Mary her inspiration and model.

The assertion: "Jesus was born of the Virgin Mary" already implies in this event a transcendent mystery, which can find its most complete expression only in the truth of Jesus' divine sonship. The truth of Mary's divine motherhood is closely tied to this central statement of the Christian faith: she is indeed the Mother of the incarnate Word, in whom is "God from God... true God from true God."

The title "Mother of God," already attested by Matthew in the equivalent expression "Mother of Emmanuel," God-with-us (cf. Mt 1:23), was explicitly attributed to Mary only after a reflection that embraced about two centuries. Third-century Christians in Egypt began to invoke Mary as *Theotókos,* Mother of God.

With this title, which is broadly echoed in the devotion of the Christian people, Mary is seen in the true dimension of her motherhood: she is the Mother of God's Son, whom she virginally begot according to his human nature and raised with her motherly love, thus contributing to the human growth of the divine person who came to transform the destiny of mankind.

In a highly significant way, the most ancient prayer to Mary (*Sub tuum praesidium...* We fly to your protection...) contains the invocation *Theotókos,* Mother of God. This title did not originally come from the reflection of theologians, but from an intuition of faith of the Christian people. Those who acknowledge Jesus as God address Mary as the Mother of God and hope to obtain her powerful aid in the trials of life.

The Council of Ephesus in 431 defined the dogma of the divine motherhood, officially attributing to Mary the title *Theotókos* in reference to the one person of Christ, true God and true man. The three expressions which the Church has used down the centuries to describe her faith in the motherhood of Mary—"Mother of Jesus," "Virgin Mother" and "Mother of God"—thus show that Mary's motherhood is intimately linked with the mystery of the Incarnation. They are affirmations of doctrine, connected as well with popular piety, which help define the identity of Christ.

General audience of September 13, 1995

Mary Was United to Jesus on the Cross

Saying that "the Virgin Mary...is acknowledged and honored as being truly the Mother of God and Mother of the Redeemer" (*LG* 53), the Council drew attention to the link between Mary's motherhood and redemption.

After becoming aware of the maternal role of Mary, who was venerated in the teaching and worship of the first centuries as the virginal Mother of Jesus Christ and therefore as the Mother of God, in the Middle Ages the Church's piety and theological reflection brought to light her cooperation in the Savior's work.

This delay is explained by the fact that the efforts of the Church Fathers and of the early ecumenical councils, focused as they were on Christ's identity, necessarily left other aspects of dogma aside. Only gradually could the revealed truth be unfolded in all its richness. Down the centuries, Mariology would always take its direction from Christology. The divine motherhood of Mary was itself proclaimed at the Council of Ephesus primarily to affirm the oneness of Christ's person. Similarly, there was a deeper understanding of Mary's presence in salvation history.

At the end of the second century, St. Irenaeus, a disciple of Polycarp, already pointed out Mary's contribution to the work of salvation. He understood the value of Mary's consent at the time of the annunciation, recognizing in the Virgin of Nazareth's obedience to and faith in the angel's message the perfect antithesis of Eve's disobedience and disbelief, with a beneficial effect on humanity's destiny. Just as Eve caused death, so Mary, with her "yes," became "a cause of salvation" for herself and for all mankind (cf. *Adv. Haer.,* III, 22, 4; *SC* 211, 441). But this affirmation was not developed in a consistent and systematic way by the other Fathers of the Church.

Instead, this doctrine was systematically worked out for the first time at the end of the 10th century in the *Life of Mary* by a Byzantine monk, John the Geometer. Here Mary is united to Christ in the whole work of redemption according to God's plan, sharing in the cross and suffering for our salvation. She remained united to the Son "in every deed, attitude and wish" (cf. *Life of Mary,* Bol. 196, f. 122 v.).

Mary's association with Jesus' saving work came about through her Mother's love, a love inspired by grace, which conferred a higher power on it. Love freed of passion proves to be the most compassionate (cf. *ibid.,* Bol. 196, f. 123 v.).

In the West St. Bernard, who died in 1153, turned to Mary and commented on the presentation of Jesus in the temple: "Offer your Son, sacrosanct virgin, and present the fruit of your womb to the Lord. For our reconciliation with all, offer the heavenly victim pleasing to God" *(Serm. 3 in Purif.,* 2: *PL* 183, 370).

A disciple and friend of St. Bernard, Arnold of Chartres, shed light especially on Mary's offering in the sacrifice of Calvary. He distinguished in the cross "two altars: one in Mary's heart, the other in Christ's body. Christ sacrificed his flesh, Mary her soul." Mary sacrificed herself spiritually in deep communion with Christ, and implored the world's salvation: "What the Mother asks, the Son approves and the Father grants" (cf. *De septem verbis Domini in cruce,* 3: *PL* 189,

1694). From this age on, other authors explained the doctrine of Mary's special cooperation in the redemptive sacrifice.

At the same time, in Christian worship and piety contemplative reflection on Mary's "compassion" developed, poignantly depicted in images of the *Pietà.* Mary's sharing in the drama of the cross makes this event more deeply human and helps the faithful to enter into the mystery; the Mother's compassion more clearly reveals the passion of the Son.

By sharing in Christ's redemptive work, Mary's spiritual and universal motherhood is also recognized. In the East, John the Geometer told Mary: "You are our mother." Giving Mary thanks "for the sorrow and suffering she bore for us," John shed light on her maternal affection and motherly regard for all those who receive salvation (cf. *Farewell Discourse on the Dormition of Our Most Glorious Lady...Mother of God,* in A. Wenger, *L'Assomption de le Très Sainte Vierge dans la tradition byzantine,* p. 407).

In the West too, the doctrine of the spiritual motherhood developed with St. Anselm, who asserted: "You are the mother...of reconciliation and the reconciled, the mother of salvation and the saved" (cf. *Oratio* 52, 8: *PL* 158, 957 *A*). Mary does not cease to be venerated as the Mother of God, but the fact that she is our Mother gives her divine motherhood a new aspect that opens within us the way to a more intimate communion with her.

Mary's motherhood in our regard does not only consist of an affective bond. Because of her merits and her intercession she contributes effectively to our spiritual birth and to the development of the life of grace within us. This is why Mary is called "Mother of grace" and "Mother of Life."

The title "Mother of Life," already employed by St. Gregory of Nyssa, was explained as follows by Bl. Guerric of Igny, who died in 1157: "She is the Mother of the Life from whom all men take life: in giving birth to this life herself, she has somehow given rebirth to all those who have lived it. Only one was begotten, but we have all been reborn" (*In Assumpt.* I, 2: *PL* 185, 188).

A 13th century text, the *Mariale,* used a vivid image in attributing this rebirth to the "painful travail" of Calvary, by which "she became the spiritual mother of the whole human race." Indeed, "in her chaste womb she conceived by compassion the children of the Church" (q. 29, par. 3).

After stating that Mary "in a wholly singular way cooperated in the work of the Savior," the Second Vatican Council concluded that for this reason, "She is our Mother in the order of grace" (*LG* 61). Thus, the Council confirmed the Church's perception that Mary is at the side of her Son as the spiritual Mother of all humanity.

Mary is our Mother. This consoling truth, offered to us ever more clearly and profoundly by the love and faith of the Church, has sustained and sustains the spiritual life of us all, and encourages us, even in suffering, to have faith and hope.

General audience of October 25, 1995

The Church Grew
in Understanding Mary's Role

In our preceding catecheses we saw how the doctrine of Mary's motherhood passed from its first formula, "Mother of Jesus," to the more complete and explicit, "Mother of God," even to the affirmation of her maternal involvement in the redemption of humanity.

For other aspects of Marian doctrine as well, many centuries were necessary to arrive at the explicit definition of the revealed truths concerning Mary. The dogmas of the immaculate conception and the assumption are typical examples of this faith journey toward the ever deeper discovery of Mary's role in the history of salvation. As we know, these dogmas were proclaimed by two of my venerable predecessors, respectively, the Servant of God Pius IX in 1854, and the Servant of God Pius XII during the jubilee year of 1950.

Mariology is a particular field of theological research. In it the Christian people's love for Mary intuited, frequently in anticipation, certain aspects of the mystery of the Blessed Virgin, calling the attention of theologians and pastors to them.

We must recognize that, at first sight, the Gospels offer scant information on the person and life of Mary. We would certainly like to have had fuller information about her, which would have enabled us to know the Mother of God better. This expectation remains unsatisfied even in the other New Testament writings, where an explicit doctrinal development regarding Mary is lacking. Even St. Paul's letters, which offer us a rich reflection on Christ and his work, limit themselves to stating, in a very significant passage, that God sent his Son "born of woman" (Gal 4:4).

Very little is said about Mary's family. If we exclude the infancy narratives, in the synoptic Gospels we find only two statements which shed some light on Mary: one concerns the attempt by his "brethren" or relatives to take Jesus back to Nazareth (cf. Mk 3:21; Mt 12:48); the other is in response to a woman's exclamation about the blessedness of Jesus' Mother (Lk 11:27).

Nevertheless, Luke, in the infancy Gospel, in the episodes of the annunciation, the visitation, the birth of Jesus, the presentation of the child in the Temple and his finding among the teachers at the age of twelve, not only provides us with some important facts, but presents a sort of "proto-Mariology" of fundamental interest. Matthew indirectly compiles this information in the account of the annunciation to Joseph (Mt 1:18–25), but only with regard to the virginal conception of Jesus.

Moreover, John's Gospel deepens our knowledge of the value for salvation history of the role the Mother of Jesus played, when it records her presence at the beginning and end of Jesus' public life. Mary's presence at the cross is especially significant. Then she received from her dying Son the charge to be mother to the beloved disciple and, in him, to all Christians (cf. Jn 2:1–12; Jn 19:25–27). Lastly, the Acts of the Apostles expressly numbers the Mother of Jesus among the women of the first community awaiting Pentecost (cf. Acts 1:14).

However, in the absence of further New Testament evidence and reliable historical sources, we know nothing of Mary's life after the Pentecost event, nor of the date and circumstances of her death. We can only suppose that she continued to live with the Apostle John and that she was very closely involved in the development of the first Christian community.

The sparse information on Mary's earthly life is compensated by its quality and theological richness, which contemporary exegesis has carefully brought to light. Moreover, we must remember that the evangelists' viewpoint is totally Christological and is concerned with the Mother only in relation to the joyful proclamation of the Son. As St. Ambrose observed, the evangelist, in expounding the mystery of the Incarnation, "believed it was better not to seem the defender of the Virgin rather than the preacher of the mystery" (*Exp. in Lucam,* 2, 6: *PL* 15, 1555).

We can recognize in this fact a special intention of the Holy Spirit. He desired to awaken in the Church an effort of research which, preserving the centrality of the mystery of Christ, might not be caught up in details about Mary's life. Its aim, above all, is to discover her role in the work of salvation, her personal holiness and her maternal mission in Christian life.

The Holy Spirit guides the Church's effort, committing her to take on Mary's own attitudes. Luke notes in the account of Jesus' birth how his mother kept all these things, "pondering them in her heart" (Lk 2:19). That is, she strove to "put together" *(symballousa),* in a deeper vision, all the events of which she was the privileged witness.

Similarly, the People of God are also urged by the same Spirit to understand deeply all that has been said about Mary, in order to progress in the knowledge of her mission, intimately linked to the mystery of Christ.

As Mariology develops, the particular role of the Christian people emerges. They cooperate, by the affirmation and witness of their faith, in the progress of Marian doctrine. Normally this progress is not only the work of theologians, even if their task is indispensable to deepening and clearly explaining the datum of faith and the Christian experience itself.

Jesus admired and praised the faith of the simple, and recognized in it a marvelous expression of the Father's benevolence (cf. Mt 11:25; Lk 10:21). Down the centuries it continues to proclaim the marvels of the history of salvation, hidden from the wise. This faith, in harmony with the Virgin's simplicity, has led to progress in the recognition of her personal holiness and the transcendent value of her motherhood.

The mystery of Mary commits every Christian, in communion with the Church, "to pondering in his heart" what the Gospel revelation affirms about the Mother of Christ. In the logic of the *Magnificat,* after the example of Mary, each one will personally experience God's love and will discover a sign of God's tenderness for us in the marvels wrought by the Blessed Trinity in the woman "full of grace."

General audience of November 8, 1995

To Honor Mary Is to Go to Jesus

After following in our previous catecheses how the Christian community's reflection on the figure and role of the Blessed Virgin in salvation history took shape from the earliest times, let us pause today to meditate on the Marian experience of the Church.

The development of Mariological thought and devotion to the Blessed Virgin down the centuries has contributed to revealing ever better the Church's Marian aspect. Of course, the Blessed Virgin is totally related to Christ, the foundation of faith and ecclesial experience, and she leads to him. That is why, in obedience to Jesus, who reserved a very special role for his Mother in the economy of salvation, Christians have venerated, loved and prayed to Mary in a most particular and fervent way. They have attributed to her an important place in faith and piety, recognizing her as the privileged way to Christ, the supreme Mediator.

The Church's Marian dimension is thus an undeniable element in the experience of the Christian people. It is expressed in many ways in the lives of believers, testifying to the place Mary holds in their hearts. It is not a superficial sentiment but a deep and conscious emotional bond, rooted in the faith which spurred Christians of the past and spurs those of the present to turn habitually to Mary, to enter a more intimate communion with Christ.

After the most ancient prayer, formulated in Egypt by the Christian communities of the third century, to implore "the Mother of God" for protection in danger, numerous invocations were addressed to her, whom the baptized consider most powerful in her intercession with the Lord.

Today, the most common prayer is the Hail Mary, whose first part consists of words from the Gospel (cf. Lk 1:28, 42). Christians learn to recite it at home from their earliest years and receive it as a precious gift to be preserved throughout life. This same prayer, repeated tens of times in the rosary, helps many of the faithful to enter into prayerful contemplation of the gospel mysteries and sometimes to remain for long intervals in intimate contact with the Mother of Jesus. Since the Middle Ages, the Hail Mary has been the most common prayer of all believers who ask the Holy Mother of the Lord to guide and protect them on their daily journey through life (cf. *MC* 42–55).

Christian people have also expressed their love for Mary by multiplying expressions of their devotion: hymns, prayers and poetic compositions, simple or sometimes of great quality, imbued with that same love for her whom the crucified one gave us as mother. Some of these, such as the "Akathistos Hymn" and the "Salve Regina," have deeply marked the faith life of believers.

The counterpart of Marian piety is the immensely rich artistic production in the East and West, which has enabled entire generations to appreciate Mary's spiritual beauty. Painters, sculptors, musicians and poets have left us masterpieces which, in shedding light on the various aspects of the Blessed Virgin's greatness, help to give us a better understanding of the meaning and value of her lofty contribution to the work of redemption. In Mary, Christian art recognizes the fulfillment of a new humanity which corresponds to God's plan and is therefore a sublime sign of hope for the whole human race.

Christians called to a vocation of special consecration could not fail to grasp this message. Mary is especially venerated in religious orders and congregations, in institutes or associations of consecrated life. Many institutes, primarily but not only feminine, include Mary's name in their titles. Nevertheless, over and above its external expressions, the spirituality of religious families, as well as of many ecclesial movements, some of which are specifically Marian, highlight their special bond with Mary as the guarantee of a charism fully and authentically lived.

This Marian reference in the lives of people especially favored by the Holy Spirit has also developed the mystical dimension. This shows how Christians can experience Mary's intervention in the innermost depths of their being. This reference to Mary binds not only committed Christians but also simple believers and even the "distant," for whom it is often their only link with the life of the Church. Pilgrimages to Marian shrines, which attract large crowds of the faithful throughout the year, are a sign of the Christian people's common sentiment for the Mother of the Lord. Some of these bulwarks of Marian piety are famous, such as Lourdes, Fatima, Loreto, Pompei, Guadalupe and Czestochowa. Others are known only at the national or local level. In all of them, the memory of events associated with recourse to Mary conveys the message of her motherly tenderness, opening our hearts to God's grace.

These places of Marian prayer are a wonderful testimony to God's mercy, which reaches man through Mary's intercession. The miracles of physical healing, spiritual redemption and conversion are the obvious sign that, with Christ and in the Spirit, Mary is continuing her work as helper and mother.

Marian shrines often become centers of evangelization. Indeed, even in the Church today, as in the community awaiting Pentecost, prayer with Mary spurs many Christians to the apostolate and to the service of their brothers and sisters. Here I would especially like to recall the great influence of Marian piety on the practice of charity and the works of mercy. Encouraged by Mary's presence, believers have often felt the need to dedicate themselves to the poor, the unfortunate and the sick, in order to be for the lowliest of the earth a sign of the motherly protection of the Blessed Virgin, the living icon of the Father's mercy.

It can clearly be seen from all this how the Marian dimension pervades the Church's whole life. The proclamation of the Word, the liturgy, the various charitable and cultural expressions find in Mary an occasion for enrichment and renewal.

The People of God, under the guidance of their pastors, are called to discern in this fact the action of the Holy Spirit who has spurred the Christian faith onward in its discovery of Mary's face. It is he who works marvels in the centers of Marian piety. It is he who, by encouraging knowledge of and love for Mary, leads the faithful to learn from the virgin of the Magnificat how to read the signs of God in history and to acquire a wisdom that makes every man and every woman the architects of a new humanity.

General audience of November 15, 1995

Mary Is a Model of Persevering Silence

After reflecting on the Marian dimension of ecclesial life, we are now going to cast light on the immense spiritual wealth Mary communicates to the Church by her example and her intercession. We would first like to pause and briefly reflect on some significant aspects of Mary's personality, which offer all believers valuable guidance in accepting and fulfilling their own vocation.

Mary has gone before us on the way of faith. Believing the angel's message, she was the first to welcome the mystery of the Incarnation and did so perfectly (cf. *RM* 13). Her journey as a believer began even earlier than her divine motherhood and developed more deeply throughout her earthly experience. Hers was a daring faith. At the annunciation she believed in what was humanly impossible. At Cana she urged Jesus to work his first miracle, pressing him to manifest his messianic powers (cf. Jn 2:1–5). Mary teaches Christians to live their faith as a demanding and engaging journey which, in every age and situation of life, requires courage and constant perseverance.

Mary's docility to the divine will was linked to her faith. Believing in God's Word, she could accept it fully in her life. Showing herself receptive to God's sovereign plan, she accepted all that was asked of her from on high. Our Lady's presence in the Church thus encourages Christians to listen to the Word of the Lord every day, to understand his loving plan in various daily events, and to cooperate faithfully in bringing it about.

This is how Mary teaches the community of believers to look to the future with total abandonment to God. In the Virgin's personal experience, hope is enriched with ever new reasons. Since the annunciation, Mary concentrates the expectations of ancient Israel on the Son of God, incarnate in her virginal womb. Her hope was strengthened during the successive stages of Jesus' hidden life in Nazareth and his public ministry. Her great faith in the word of Christ, who had announced his resurrection on the third day, prevented her from wavering, even when faced with the drama of the cross. She retained her hope in the fulfillment of the messianic work, and after the darkness of Good Friday, awaited steadfastly the morning of the resurrection.

On their difficult path through history, between the "already" of salvation received and the "not yet" of its fulfillment, believers know they can count on the help of the "Mother of Hope." After experiencing Christ's victory over the powers of death, she communicates to them an ever new capacity to await God's future and to abandon themselves to the Lord's promises.

Mary's example enables the Church to appreciate better the value of silence. Mary's silence is not only moderation in speech. It is especially a wise capacity for remembering and embracing in a single gaze of faith the mystery of the Word made man and the events of his earthly life. Mary passes on to believers this silence as acceptance of the Word, this ability to meditate on the mystery of Christ. In a noisy world filled with messages of all kinds, her witness fosters a contemplative spirit and enables us to appreciate a spiritually rich silence.

Mary witnesses to the value of a humble and hidden life. Everyone usually demands, and sometimes almost claims, to be able to realize fully his own person and qualities. Everyone is sensitive to esteem and honor. The Gospels often mention that the apostles were ambitious for the most important places in the kingdom and they argued among themselves as to which of them was the greatest. In this matter Jesus had to teach them the need for humility and service (cf. Mt 18:1–5; 20:20–28; Mk 9:33–37; 10:35–45; Lk 9:46–48; 22:24–27). Mary, on the contrary, never sought honor or the advantages of a privileged position. She always tried to fulfill God's will, leading a life according to the Father's plan of salvation. To all those who often feel the burden of a seemingly insignificant life, Mary reveals how valuable life can be if it is lived for love of Christ and one's brothers and sisters.

Mary also witnesses to the value of a life that is pure and full of tenderness for all people. The beauty of her soul, totally offered to the Lord, is an object of admiration for the Christian people. In Mary, the Christian community has always seen the ideal woman, full of love and tenderness because she lived in purity of mind and body. The cynicism of a certain contemporary culture too often seems not to recognize the value of chastity and degrades sexuality by separating it from personal dignity and God's plan. In face of this, the Virgin Mary holds up the witness of a purity that illumines the conscience and leads to a greater love for creatures and for the Lord.

Furthermore, Mary appears to Christians of all times as the one who feels deep compassion for the sufferings of humanity. This compassion does not consist only in an emotional sympathy, but is expressed in effective and concrete help when confronted with humanity's material and moral misery. In following Mary, the Church is called to take on the same attitude toward all the earth's poor and suffering. The maternal attention of the Lord's Mother to the tears, sorrows and hardships of men and women of all ages must spur Christians, especially at the dawn of the new millennium, to increase the concrete and visible signs of a love that will enable today's humble and suffering people to share in the promises and hopes of the new world which is born from Easter.

Human affection for and devotion to the Mother of Jesus surpass the Church's visible boundaries and foster sentiments of reconciliation. As a mother, Mary desires the union of all her children. Her presence in the Church is an invitation to preserve the unanimity of heart which reigned in the first community (cf. Acts 1:14), and consequently, to seek ways of unity and peace among all men and women of goodwill. In interceding with her Son, Mary asks the grace of unity for all humanity, in view of building a civilization of love, overcoming tendencies to division, temptations to revenge and hatred, and the perverse fascination of violence.

Our Lady's motherly smile, reproduced in so much Marian iconography, expresses a fullness of grace and peace that seeks to be shared. This expression of her serenity of spirit effectively contributes to giving the Church a joyful face.

Welcoming in the annunciation the angel's invitation to "rejoice" (*chaïré*=rejoice: Lk 1:28), Mary was the first to share in the messianic joy foretold by the prophets for the "Daughter of Zion" (cf. Is 12:6; Zep 3:14–15; Zec 9:9). She passes it on to humanity in every age.

Invoking her as *causa nostrae laetitiae,* the Christian people find in her the capacity to communicate the joy that is born of hope, even in the midst of life's trials, and to guide those who commend themselves to her to the joy that knows no end.

General audience of November 22, 1995

Mary Shows Us
God's Respect for Woman

The theological and spiritual aspects of the Church's teaching on Mary, which have been amply developed in our century, have recently acquired a new importance from the sociological and pastoral standpoint. This is also due to a clearer understanding of woman's role in the Christian community and in society, as we see in many significant interventions of the magisterium.

The message which the Council Fathers addressed to women at the conclusion of Vatican II on December 8, 1965 is well known: "But the hour is coming, in fact has come, when the vocation of woman is being achieved in its fullness, the hour in which woman acquires in the world an influence, an effect and a power never hitherto achieved" (*Enchiridion Vat.*, I, 307).

I confirmed these affirmations a few years later in the Apostolic Letter *Mulieris Dignitatem:* "The dignity and vocation of women—a subject of constant human and Christian reflection—have gained exceptional prominence in recent years" (n. 1).

The role and dignity of woman have been especially championed in this century by the feminist movement. It has sought to react, sometimes in forceful ways, against everything in the past and present that has hindered the full appreciation and development of the feminine personality as well as woman's participation in the many expressions of social and political life.

These demands were in large part legitimate and contributed to building up a more balanced view of the feminine question in the contemporary world. The Church, especially in recent times, has paid special attention to these demands, encouraged by the fact that the figure of Mary, if seen in the light of her Gospel life, is a valid response to woman's desire for emancipation. Mary is the only human person who eminently fulfills God's plan of love for humanity.

This plan was already manifest in the Old Testament, with the creation narrative that introduces the first couple created in the image of God himself: "So God created man in his own image, in the image of God he created him; male and female he created them" (Gn 1:27). Thus woman, no less than man, bears God's image in herself. This means that, since her appearance on the earth as a result of the divine action, she too is appreciated: "God saw everything that he had made, and behold, it was very good" (Gn 1:31). According to this view, the difference between man and woman does not imply the inferiority of the latter nor her inequality. It is a new element which enriches God's plan, and is "very good."

However, God's intention goes well beyond what is revealed in Genesis. In Mary, God created a feminine personality which greatly surpasses the ordinary condition of woman as it appears in the creation of Eve. Mary's perfection and her unique excellence in the world of grace are fruits of the particular divine benevolence which seeks to raise everyone, men and women, to the moral perfection and holiness which are proper to the adopted children of God. Mary is "blessed among women"; however, every woman shares in some way in her sublime dignity in the divine plan. The remarkable gift to the Mother of the Lord not only testifies to what we could call

God's respect for woman, but also emphasizes the profound regard in God's plans for her irreplaceable role in human history.

Women need to discover this divine esteem in order to be ever more aware of their lofty dignity. The historical and social situations which caused the reaction of feminism were marked by a lack of appreciation of woman's worth; frequently she was relegated to a second rate or even marginal role. This did not allow her to express fully the wealth of intelligence and wisdom contained in her femininity. Indeed, throughout history women have often suffered from scant esteem for their abilities, and sometimes even scorn and unjust prejudice. Despite important changes, this state of affairs unfortunately continues even today in many nations and parts of the world. The figure of Mary shows that God has such esteem for woman that any form of discrimination lacks a theoretical basis.

The marvelous work which the Creator achieved in Mary gives men and women the possibility to discover dimensions of their condition which before were not sufficiently perceived. In beholding the Mother of the Lord, women will be able to understand better their dignity and the greatness of their mission. In the light of the virgin Mother, men too will be able to acquire a fuller and more balanced view of their identity, of the family and of society.

Attentive consideration of the figure of Mary, as she is presented to us in Sacred Scripture as the Church reads it in faith, is still more necessary in view of the disparagement she sometimes receives from certain feminist currents. In some cases, the Virgin of Nazareth has been presented as the symbol of the female personality imprisoned in a narrow, confining domesticity.

On the contrary, Mary is the model of the full development of woman's vocation. Despite the objective limits imposed by her special condition, she exercised a vast influence on the destiny of humanity and the transformation of society.

Moreover, Marian doctrine can shed light on the multiple ways in which the life of grace promotes woman's spiritual beauty. In view of the shameful exploitation that sometimes makes woman an object without dignity, destined for the satisfaction of base passions, Mary reaffirms the sublime meaning of feminine beauty, a gift and reflection of God's beauty.

Feminine perfection, as it was fully realized in Mary, can at first sight seem to be an exceptional case and impossible to imitate, a model too lofty for imitation. The unique holiness of Mary, who from the very first moment received the privilege of the immaculate conception, is sometimes considered unreachably distant.

However, far from being a restraint on the way of following the Lord, Mary's exalted holiness is destined in God's plan to encourage all Christians to open themselves to the sanctifying power of the grace of God, for whom nothing is impossible. Therefore, in Mary all are called to put total trust in the divine omnipotence which transforms hearts, guiding them toward full receptivity to his providential plan of love.

General audience of November 29, 1995

Mary Sheds Light on the Role of Woman

As I have already explained in the preceding catecheses, the role entrusted to Mary in the divine plan of salvation sheds light on woman's vocation in the life of the Church and society by defining its difference in relation to man. The model Mary represents clearly shows what is specific to the feminine personality.

To advance woman's emancipation, recently some trends in the feminist movement have sought to make her like man in every way. However, the divine intention manifested in creation, though desiring woman to be man's equal in dignity and worth, at the same time clearly affirms her diversity and specific features. Woman's identity cannot consist in being a copy of man, since she is endowed with her own qualities and prerogatives. These give her a particular uniqueness that is always to be fostered and encouraged.

These prerogatives and particular features of the feminine personality attained their full development in Mary. The fullness of divine grace actually fostered in her all the natural abilities typical of woman.

Mary's role in the work of salvation totally depends on Christ's. It is a unique function, required by the fulfillment of the mystery of the Incarnation. Mary's motherhood was necessary to give the world its Savior, the true Son of God, and also perfectly man.

The importance of woman's cooperation in the coming of Christ is emphasized by God's initiative. Through the angel, God communicated his plan of salvation to the Virgin of Nazareth so that she could consciously and freely cooperate by giving her own generous consent. Here the loftiest model of woman's collaboration in the redemption of man—every man—is fulfilled. This model represents the transcendent reference point for every affirmation of woman's role and function in history.

In carrying out this sublime form of cooperation, Mary also showed the style in which woman must concretely express her mission. With regard to the angel's message, the Virgin made no proud demands nor did she seek to satisfy personal ambitions. Luke presents her to us as wanting only to offer her humble service with total and trusting acceptance of the divine plan of salvation. This is the meaning of her response: "Behold, I am the handmaid of the Lord; let it be to me according to your word" (Lk 1:38).

It is not a question of a purely passive acceptance, since her consent is given only after she has expressed the difficulty that arose from her intent to remain a virgin, inspired by her will to belong more completely to the Lord. Having received the angel's response, Mary immediately expresses her readiness, maintaining an attitude of humble service. It is the humble, valuable service that so many women, following Mary's example, have offered and continue to offer in the Church for the growth of Christ's kingdom.

The figure of Mary reminds women today of the value of motherhood. In the contemporary world an appropriate and balanced importance is not always given to this value. In some cases, the need for women to work in order to provide for the needs of their families, and an erroneous concept of freedom, which sees child care as a hindrance to woman's autonomy and opportunities, have obscured the significance of motherhood for the development of the feminine personality. On the contrary, in other cases the biological aspect of childbirth becomes so important as to overshadow the other significant opportunities woman has for expressing her innate vocation to be a mother.

In Mary we have been given to understand the true meaning of motherhood, which attains its loftiest dimension in the divine plan of salvation. For her, being a mother not only endows her feminine personality, directed toward the gift of life, with its full development. It also represents an answer of faith to woman's own vocation, which assumes its truest value only in the light of God's covenant (cf. *MD* 19).

In looking attentively at Mary, we also discover in her the model of virginity lived for the kingdom. The virgin *par excellence,* in her heart she grew in her desire to live in this state in order to achieve an ever deeper intimacy with God. For women called to virginal chastity, Mary reveals the lofty meaning of so special a vocation. Thus she draws attention to the spiritual fruitfulness which it produces in the divine plan: a higher order of motherhood, a motherhood according to the Spirit (cf. *MD* 21).

Mary's maternal heart, open to all human misfortune, also reminds women that the development of the feminine personality calls for a commitment to charity. More sensitive to the values of the heart, woman shows a high capacity for personal self-giving. To all in our age who offer selfish models for affirming the feminine personality, the luminous and holy figure of the Lord's Mother shows that authentic fulfillment of the divine plan for one's own life is possible only by self-giving and self-forgetfulness.

Mary's presence, therefore, encourages sentiments of mercy and solidarity in women for situations of human distress. She arouses a desire to alleviate the pain of those who suffer: the poor, the sick and all who need help. In virtue of her special bond with Mary, woman has often throughout history represented God's closeness to the expectations of goodness and tenderness of humanity wounded by hatred and sin, by sowing in the world seeds of a civilization that can respond to violence with love.

General audience of December 6, 1995

The Council's Teaching on Mary Is Rich and Positive

Today I would like to reflect on the particular presence of the Mother of the Church at what was certainly the most important ecclesial event of our century: the Second Vatican Ecumenical Council. Pope John XXIII opened it on the morning of October 11, 1962 and Pope Paul VI closed it on December 8, 1965.

An extraordinary Marian tone actually marked the Council from its beginning. In the Apostolic Letter *Celebrandi Concilii Oecumenici,* my venerable Predecessor, the Servant of God John XXIII, had already recommended recourse to the powerful intercession of Mary, "Mother of grace and heavenly patroness of the Council" (April 11, 1961, *AAS* 53 [1961], 242).

Subsequently, in 1962, on the feast of the Purification of Mary, Pope John set the opening of the Council for October 11. He explained that he had chosen this date in memory of the great Council of Ephesus, which on that date had proclaimed Mary *Theotókos,* Mother of God (Motu Proprio *Concilium; AAS* 54 [1962], 67–68). Later, in his opening address, the Pope entrusted the Council itself to the "Help of Christians, Help of Bishops," imploring her motherly assistance for the successful outcome of the Council's work (*AAS* 54 [1962], 795).

The Council Fathers also turned their thoughts expressly to Mary in their message to the world at the opening of the Council's sessions, saying: "We successors of the apostles, joined together in prayer with Mary, the Mother of Jesus, form one apostolic body" (*Acta Synodalia,* I, I, 254). Thus they linked themselves, in communion with Mary, to the early Church awaiting the Holy Spirit (cf. Acts 1:14).

At the second session of the Council it was proposed that the treatment of the Blessed Virgin Mary be put into the Constitution on the Church. This initiative, although expressly recommended by the theological commission, prompted a variety of opinions. Some considered this proposal inadequate for emphasizing the very special mission of Jesus' Mother in the Church. They maintained that only a separate document could express Mary's dignity, preeminence, exceptional holiness and unique role in the redemption accomplished by the Son. Furthermore, regarding Mary as above the Church in a certain way, they were afraid that the decision to put the Marian teaching in the treatment of the Church would not sufficiently emphasize Mary's privileges and would reduce her role to the level of other members of the Church (*Acta Synodalia,* II, III, 338–342).

Others, however, spoke in favor of the theological commission's proposal to put the doctrinal treatment of Mary and the Church in a single document. According to them, these realities could not be separated at a Council which, in aiming to rediscover the identity and mission of the People of God, had to show its close connection with the one who is the type and exemplar of the Church in her virginity and motherhood. Indeed, as an eminent member of the ecclesial community, the Blessed Virgin has a special place in the Church's doctrine. Furthermore, by stressing the link between Mary and the Church, Christians of the Reformation could better understand the Marian teaching presented by the Council (*Acta Synodalia,* II, III, 343–345).

Moved by the same love for Mary, the Council Fathers thus tended in their expression of different doctrinal positions to favor various aspects of her person. Some reflected on Mary primarily in her relationship to Christ; others considered her more as a member of the Church. After an intense doctrinal discussion attentive to the dignity of the Mother of God and to her particular presence in the Church's life, it was decided that the treatment of Mary would be situated in the Council's document on the Church (cf. *Acta Synodalia,* II, III, 627).

The new schema on the Blessed Virgin, drafted so as to be included in the *Dogmatic Constitution on the Church,* shows real doctrinal progress. The stress placed on Mary's faith and a more systematic concern to base Marian doctrine on Scripture are significant and useful elements for enriching the piety and esteem of the Christian people for the Blessed Mother of God.

Moreover, with the passing of time the danger of reductionism, feared by some Fathers, proved to be unfounded. Mary's mission and privileges were amply reaffirmed; her cooperation in the divine plan of salvation was highlighted; the harmony of this cooperation with Christ's unique mediation appeared more evident.

For the first time, the conciliar magisterium offered the Church a doctrinal exposition of Mary's role in Christ's redemptive work and in the life of the Church. Thus, we must consider the Council Fathers' choice, which proved very fruitful for later doctrinal work, to have been a truly providential decision.

During the Council's sessions, many Fathers wished further to enrich Marian doctrine with other statements on Mary's role in the work of salvation. The particular context in which Vatican II's Mariological debate took place did not allow these wishes, although substantial and widespread, to be accepted. But the Council's entire discussion of Mary remains vigorous and balanced. The topics themselves, though not fully defined, received significant attention in the overall treatment.

Thus, the hesitation of some Fathers regarding the title of Mediatrix did not prevent the Council from using this title once, and from stating in other terms Mary's mediating role from her consent to the angel's message to her motherhood in the order of grace (cf. *LG* 62). Furthermore, the Council asserted her cooperation "in a wholly singular way" in the work of restoring supernatural life to souls (*LG* 61). Lastly, even if it avoided using the title "Mother of the Church," the text of *Lumen Gentium* clearly underscores the Church's veneration for Mary as a most loving Mother.

The entire exposition in chapter eight of the *Dogmatic Constitution on the Church* clearly shows that terminological precautions did not prevent a very rich and positive presentation of basic doctrine, an expression of faith and love for Mary, whom the Church acknowledges as Mother and model. On the other hand, the Fathers' differing viewpoints, as they emerged during the conciliar debate, turned out to be providential. On the basis of their harmonious relationship, they have afforded the faith and devotion of the Christian people a more complete and balanced presentation of the marvelous identity of the Lord's Mother and of her exceptional role in the work of redemption.

General audience of December 13, 1995

Mary's Place Is the Highest after Christ

Following *Lumen Gentium,* which in chapter eight sets forth "both the role of the Blessed Virgin in the mystery of the incarnate Word and the Mystical Body, and the duties of the redeemed toward the Mother of God," in this catechesis I would like to offer a basic summary of the Church's faith in Mary. With the Council I reaffirm that I do not intend "to give a complete doctrine on Mary," nor "to decide those questions which the work of theologians has not yet fully clarified" (*LG* 54).

It is my intention first of all to describe "the role of the Blessed Virgin in the mystery of the incarnate Word and the Mystical Body" (*LG* 54) by referring to data from Scripture and the apostolic Tradition. This will take into account the doctrinal development that has taken place in the Church up to our day. Moreover, since Mary's role in the history of salvation is closely linked to the mystery of Christ and the Church, I will not lose sight of these essential reference points. By offering Marian doctrine the proper context, they enable us to discover its vast and inexhaustible riches.

Exploring the mystery of the Lord's Mother is truly vast and has occupied many pastors and theologians through the centuries. In their endeavor to point out the central aspects of

Mariology, some have at times treated it together with Christology or ecclesiology. However, taking into account her relationship with all the mysteries of faith, Mary deserves a specific treatment which highlights her person and role in the history of salvation, in the light of the Bible and of ecclesiastical tradition. It also seems useful, following the Council's directives, to explain accurately "the duties of the redeemed toward the Mother of God, who is Mother of Christ and Mother of men, particularly of the faithful" (*LG* 54).

Indeed, the part assigned to her by the divine plan of salvation requires of Christians not only acceptance and attention, but also concrete choices which express in life the gospel attitudes of Mary, who goes before the Church in faith and holiness. The Mother of the Lord is thus destined to exercise a special influence on the believer's way of praying. The Church's liturgy itself recognizes her singular place in the devotion and life of every believer.

It is necessary to emphasize that Marian teaching and devotion are not the fruit of sentimentality. The mystery of Mary is a revealed truth which imposes itself on the intellect of believers and requires of those in the Church who have the task of studying and teaching a method of doctrinal reflection no less rigorous than that used in all theology. Moreover, Jesus himself had invited his contemporaries not to be led by enthusiasm in considering his Mother, recognizing in Mary especially the one who is blessed because she listens to the Word of God and keeps it (cf. Lk 11:28). Not only affection but especially the light of the Spirit must guide us in understanding the Mother of Jesus and her contribution to the work of salvation.

With regard to the measure and balance to be maintained in both Marian doctrine and devotion, the Council strongly urged theologians and preachers of the divine word "to abstain zealously...from all gross exaggerations" (*LG* 67). This exaggeration comes from those who adopt a maximalist attitude, which seeks to extend systematically to Mary the prerogatives of Christ and all the charisms of the Church.

Instead, it is always necessary in Marian doctrine to safeguard the infinite difference existing between the human person of Mary and the divine person of Jesus. To attribute the "maximum" to Mary cannot become a norm of Mariology. It must constantly refer to the testimony of revelation regarding God's gifts to the Virgin on account of her sublime mission.

Likewise, the Council exhorted theologians and preachers to refrain from "narrow-mindedness" (*LG* 67), that is, from the danger of minimalism. This can be manifest in doctrinal positions, in exegetical interpretations and in acts of devotion which tend to reduce and almost deny Mary's importance in the history of salvation, her perpetual virginity and her holiness.

Such extreme positions should always be avoided through a consistent and sincere fidelity to revealed truth as expressed in Scripture and in the apostolic Tradition. The Council itself offers us a criterion for discerning authentic Marian doctrine: Mary "occupies a place in the Church which is the highest after Christ and yet very close to us" (*LG* 54).

The *highest* place: we must discover this lofty position granted to Mary in the mystery of salvation. However, it is a question of a vocation totally in relationship to Christ. The place *closest to us:* our life is profoundly influenced by Mary's example and intercession. Nonetheless, we must ask ourselves about our effort to be close to her. The entire teaching of salvation history invites us to look to the Virgin. Christian asceticism in every age invites us to think of her as a model of perfect adherence to the Lord's will. The chosen model of holiness, Mary guides the steps of believers on their journey to heaven.

Through her closeness to the events of our daily history, Mary sustains us in trials. She encourages us in difficulty, always pointing out to us the goal of eternal salvation. Thus, her role as Mother is seen ever more clearly: Mother of her Son Jesus, tender and vigilant Mother to each one of us, to whom, from the cross, the Redeemer entrusted her, that we might welcome her as children in faith.

General audience of January 3, 1996

Mary's Relationship with the Trinity

Chapter eight of *Lumen Gentium* shows in the mystery of Christ the absolutely necessary reference to Marian doctrine. In this regard, the first words of the introduction are significant: "Wishing in his supreme goodness and wisdom to effect the redemption of the world, 'when the fullness of time came, God sent his Son, born of a woman...that we might receive the adoption of sons' (Gal 4:4–5)" (*LG* 52). This Son is the Messiah awaited by the people of the Old Covenant, sent by the Father at a decisive moment of history, the "fullness of time" (Gal 4:4), which coincides with his birth in our world from a woman. She who brought the eternal Son of God to humanity can never be separated from him who is found at the center of the divine plan carried out in history.

The primacy of Christ is shown forth in the Church, his Mystical Body. In it the faithful are "joined to Christ the head...in the unity of fellowship with all his saints" (*LG* 52). Christ draws all men to himself. Since in her maternal role she is closely united with her Son, Mary helps direct the gaze and heart of believers toward him.

She is the way that leads to Christ. Indeed, she who "at the message of the angel received the Word of God in her heart and in her body" (*LG* 53) shows us how to receive into our lives the Son come down from heaven, teaching us to make Jesus the center and the supreme "law" of our existence.

Mary also helps us discover, at the origin of the whole work of salvation, the sovereign action of the Father who calls men to become sons in the one Son. Recalling the very beautiful expressions of Ephesians: "God, who is rich in mercy out of the great love with which he loved us, even when we were dead through our trespasses, made us alive together with Christ" (Eph 2:4), the Council gives God the title "most wonderful": the Son "born of a woman" is thus seen as the fruit of the Father's mercy and enables us to understand better how this woman is the "Mother of mercy."

In the same context, the Council also calls God "most wise," suggesting a particular attention to the close link between Mary and the divine wisdom, which in its mysterious plan willed the Virgin's motherhood.

The Council's text also reminds us of the unique bond uniting Mary with the Holy Spirit, using the words of the Nicene-Constantinopolitan Creed which we recite in the Eucharistic liturgy: "For us men and for our salvation he came down from heaven; by the power of the Holy Spirit he was born of the Virgin Mary, and became man." In expressing the unchanging faith of the Church, the Council reminds us that the marvelous Incarnation of the Son took place in the Virgin Mary's womb without man's cooperation, by the power of the Holy Spirit.

The introduction to chapter eight of *Lumen Gentium* thus shows in a Trinitarian perspective an essential dimension of Marian doctrine. Everything comes from the will of the Father, who has sent his Son into the world, revealing him to men and establishing him as the head of the Church and the center of history. This plan was fulfilled by the Incarnation, the work of the Holy Spirit, but with the essential cooperation of a woman, the Virgin Mary. She thus became an integral part in the economy of communicating the Trinity to the human race.

Mary's threefold relationship with the divine persons is confirmed in precise words and with a description of the characteristic relationship which links the Mother of the Lord to the Church: "She is endowed with the high office and dignity of being the Mother of the Son of God, by which account she is also the beloved daughter of the Father and the temple of the Holy Spirit" (*LG* 53). Mary's fundamental dignity is that of being "Mother of the Son," which is expressed in Christian doctrine and devotion with the title "Mother of God."

This is a surprising term, which shows the humility of God's only-begotten Son in his Incarnation and, in connection with it, the most high privilege granted a creature who was called to give him birth in the flesh. Mother of the Son, Mary is the "beloved daughter of the Father" in a unique way. She has been granted an utterly special likeness between her motherhood and the divine fatherhood.

Again, every Christian is a "temple of the Holy Spirit," according to the Apostle Paul's expression (cf. 1 Cor 6:19). But this assertion takes on an extraordinary meaning in Mary. In her the relationship with the Holy Spirit is enriched with a spousal dimension. I recalled this in the Encyclical *Redemptoris Mater:* "The Holy Spirit had already come down upon her, and she became his faithful spouse at the annunciation, welcoming the Word of the true God..." (n. 26).

Mary's privileged relationship with the Trinity therefore confers on her a dignity which far surpasses that of every other creature. The Council recalled this explicitly: because of this "gift of sublime grace" Mary "far surpasses all creatures" (*LG* 53). However, this most high dignity does not hinder Mary's solidarity with each of us.

Lumen Gentium goes on to say that "because she belongs to the offspring of Adam she is one with all those who are to be saved." She has been redeemed, in a more exalted fashion, "by reason of the merits of her Son" (*LG* 53).

Here we see the authentic meaning of Mary's privileges and of her extraordinary relationship with the Trinity. Their purpose is to enable her to cooperate in the salvation of the human race. The immeasurable greatness of the Lord's Mother, therefore, remains a gift of God's love for all people. By proclaiming her "blessed" (Lk 1:48), generations praise the "great things" (Lk 1:49) the Almighty has done in her for humanity, "in remembrance of his mercy" (Lk 1:54).

General audience of January 10, 1996

Victory over Sin
Comes through a Woman

"The books of the Old Testament describe the history of salvation, by which the coming of Christ into the world was slowly prepared. The earliest documents, as they are read in the Church and are understood in the light of a further and full revelation, bring the figure of a woman, Mother of the Redeemer, into a gradually clearer light" (*LG* 55).

With these statements the Second Vatican Council reminds us how the figure of Mary gradually took shape from the very beginning of salvation history. She is already glimpsed in the Old Testament texts but is fully understood only when these "are read in the Church" and understood in the light of the New Testament.

By inspiring the various human authors, the Holy Spirit oriented Old Testament revelation to Christ, who was to come into the world from the Virgin Mary's womb.

Among the biblical accounts which foretold the Mother of the Redeemer, the Council particularly cites those in which God revealed his plan of salvation after the fall of Adam and Eve. The Lord says to the serpent, the personification of the spirit of evil: "I will put enmity between you and the woman, and between your seed and her seed; he shall bruise his heel" (Gn 3:15).

These statements, called the Protogospel—the first Good News—by Christian tradition since the 16th century, enable us to see God's saving will from the origins of humanity. According to the sacred author's narrative, the Lord's first reaction to sin is not to punish the guilty but to offer them the hope of salvation and to involve them actively in the work of redemption, showing his great generosity even to those who had offended him.

The Protogospel's words also reveal the unique destiny of the woman who, although yielding to the serpent's temptation before the man did, in virtue of the divine plan later became God's first ally. Eve was the serpent's accomplice in enticing man to sin. Overturning this situation, God declares that he will make the woman the serpent's enemy.

Exegetes now agree in recognizing that the text of Genesis, according to the original Hebrew, does not attribute action against the serpent directly to the woman, but to her offspring. Nevertheless, the text gives great prominence to the role she will play in the struggle against the tempter: the one who defeats the serpent will be her offspring.

Who is this woman? The biblical text does not mention her personal name but allows us to glimpse a new woman, desired by God to atone for Eve's fall. She is called to restore woman's role and dignity, and to contribute to changing humanity's destiny, cooperating through her maternal mission in God's victory over Satan.

In the light of the New Testament and the Church's tradition, we know that the new woman announced by the Protogospel is Mary, and in "her seed" we recognize her son Jesus, who triumphed over Satan's power in the Paschal Mystery.

We also observe that in Mary the enmity God put between the serpent and the woman is fulfilled in two ways. God's perfect ally and the devil's enemy, she was completely removed from Satan's domination in the immaculate conception, when she was fashioned in grace by the Holy Spirit and preserved from every stain of sin. In addition, associated with her Son's saving work, Mary was fully involved in the fight against the spirit of evil.

Thus the titles "Immaculate Conception" and "Cooperator of the Redeemer" show the lasting antagonism between the serpent and the New Eve. The Church's faith attributes these titles to Mary in order to proclaim her spiritual beauty and her intimate participation in the wonderful work of redemption.

Exegetes and theologians claim that the light of the New Eve, Mary, shines from the pages of Genesis onto the whole economy of salvation. In that text they already see the bond between Mary and the Church. Here we point out with joy that the term "woman," used in its generic form in the Genesis text, spurs women especially to join the Virgin of Nazareth and her task in the work of salvation, for they are called to take part in the fight against the spirit of evil.

Women who, like Eve, could succumb to Satan's seduction, through solidarity with Mary receive superior strength to combat the enemy, becoming God's first allies on the way of salvation. God's mysterious alliance with woman can also be seen in a variety of ways in our day: in women's assiduous personal prayer and liturgical devotion, in their catechetical service and in their witness to charity, in the many feminine vocations to the consecrated life, in religious education in the family, etc.

All these signs are a very concrete fulfillment of the Protogospel's prediction. Indeed, by suggesting a universal extension of the "woman" within and beyond the visible confines of the Church, the Protogospel shows that Mary's unique vocation is inseparable from humanity's vocation. In particular, it is inseparable from that of every woman, on which light has been shed by the mission of Mary, proclaimed God's first ally against Satan and evil.

General audience of January 24, 1996

Isaiah's Prophecy Is Fulfilled in the Incarnation

In discussing the figure of Mary in the Old Testament, the Council refers to the well known text of Isaiah, which caught the particular attention of the early Christians: "Behold, a virgin shall conceive and bear a son, and shall call his name Emmanuel" (Is 7:14; cf. *LG* 55).

During the annunciation of the angel, who invited Joseph to take to himself Mary, his wife, "for that which is conceived in her is of the Holy Spirit," Matthew gives a Christological and Marian significance to the prophecy. He adds: "All this took place to fulfill what the Lord had spoken by the prophet: 'Behold, a virgin shall conceive and bear a son, and his name shall be called Emmanuel' (which means God-with-us)" (Mt 1:22–23).

In the Hebrew text this prophecy does not explicitly foretell the virginal birth of Emmanuel: the word used *(almah)* simply means "a young woman," not necessarily a virgin. Moreover, we know that Jewish tradition did not hold up the idea of perpetual virginity, nor did it ever express the idea of virginal motherhood.

In the Greek tradition, however, the Hebrew word was translated *parthenos*—virgin. In this fact, which could seem merely a peculiarity of translation, we must recognize a mysterious orientation given by the Holy Spirit to Isaiah's words in order to prepare for the understanding of the Messiah's extraordinary birth. The translation of the word as "virgin" is explained by the fact that Isaiah's text solemnly prepares for the announcement of the conception and presents it as a divine sign (Is 7:10–14), arousing the expectation of an extraordinary conception. It is not something extraordinary for a young woman to conceive a son after being joined to her husband. However, the prophecy makes no reference to the husband. Such a formulation, then, suggested the interpretation given later in the Greek version.

In the original context, the prophecy of Isaiah 7:14 was the divine reply to a lack of faith on the part of King Ahaz. Threatened with an invasion from the armies of the neighboring kings, he sought his own salvation and that of his kingdom in Assyria's protection. In advising him to put his trust solely in God and to reject the dreadful Assyrian intervention, the prophet Isaiah invited him on the Lord's behalf to make an act of faith in God's power: "Ask a sign of the Lord your God." At the king's refusal, for he preferred to seek salvation in human aid, the prophet made the famous prediction: "Hear then, O house of David! Is it too little for you to weary men, that you weary my God also? Therefore, the Lord himself will give you a sign. Behold, a virgin shall conceive and bear a son, and shall call his name Emmanuel" (Is 7:13–14). The announcement of the sign of Emmanuel, "God-with-us," implies the promise of God's presence in history, which will find its full meaning in the mystery of the Incarnation of the Word.

In the announcement of the wondrous birth of Emmanuel, the indication of the woman who conceives and gives birth shows a certain intention to associate the mother with the destiny of the son—a prince destined to establish an ideal kingdom, the "messianic" kingdom—and offers a glimpse of a special divine plan, which highlights the woman's role. The sign is not only the child, but the extraordinary conception revealed later in the birth itself, a hope-filled event, which stresses the central role of the mother.

The prophecy of Emmanuel must also be understood in the horizon opened by the promise made to David, a promise we read about in the Second Book of Samuel. Here the prophet Nathan promises the king God's favor toward David's descendant: "He shall build a house for my name, and I will establish the throne of his kingdom forever. I will be his father, and he shall be my son" (2 Sm 7:13–14). God wants to exercise a paternal role toward David's offspring, a role that will reveal its full, authentic meaning in the New Testament with the Incarnation of the Son of God in the family of David (cf. Rom 1:3).

In another very familiar text, the same prophet Isaiah confirms the unusual nature of Emmanuel's birth. Here are his words: "For to us a child is born, to us a son is given, and the government will be upon his shoulder, and he will be called 'Wonderful Counselor, Mighty God, Everlasting Father, Prince of Peace'" (9:5). Thus, in the series of names given the child, the prophet expresses the qualities of his royal office: wisdom, might, fatherly kindness, peacemaking. The mother is no longer mentioned here, but the exaltation of the son, who brings the people all they can hope for in the messianic kingdom, is also reflected in the woman who conceived him and gave him birth.

A famous prophecy of Micah also alludes to the birth of Emmanuel. The prophet says: "But you, O Bethlehem Ephrathah, who are little to be among the clans of Judah, from you shall come forth for me one who is to be ruler in Israel, whose origin is from of old, from ancient days. Therefore, the Lord shall give them up until the time when she who is in travail has brought forth..." (5:2–3). These words reecho the expectation of a birth full of messianic hope, in which once again the mother's role is stressed, the mother explicitly remembered and ennobled by the wondrous event that brings joy and salvation.

Mary's virginal motherhood was prepared for in a more general way by God's favor to the humble and the poor (cf. *LG* 55). By their attitude of placing all their trust in the Lord, they anticipated the profound meaning of Mary's virginity. By renouncing the richness of human motherhood, she awaited from God all the fruitfulness of her own life.

The Old Testament does not contain a formal announcement of the virginal motherhood, which was fully revealed only by the New Testament. Nevertheless, Isaiah's prophecy (Is 7:14) prepared for the revelation of this mystery and was construed so in the Greek translation of the Old Testament. By quoting the prophecy thus translated, Matthew's Gospel proclaims its perfect fulfillment through the conception of Jesus in Mary's virginal womb.

General audience of January 31, 1996

Motherhood Is God's Special Gift

Motherhood is a gift of God. After giving birth to Cain, her firstborn son, Eve exclaimed, "I have gotten a man with the help of the Lord" (Gn 4:1). With these words, Genesis presents the first motherhood in human history as a grace and joy that springs from the Creator's goodness.

The birth of Isaac is similarly described at the origin of the Chosen People. God promised Abraham, who had been deprived of children and was advanced in years, descendants as numerous as the stars of heaven (cf. Gn 15:5). The patriarch welcomed the promise with the faith that revealed God's plan to this man: "He believed the Lord, and he reckoned it to him as righteousness" (Gn 15:6).

This promise was confirmed in the words the Lord spoke on the occasion of the covenant he made with Abraham: "Behold, my covenant is with you, and you shall be the father of a multitude of nations" (Gn 17:4).

Extraordinary and mysterious events emphasized how Sarah's motherhood was primarily the fruit of the mercy of God, who gives life beyond all human expectation: "I will bless her, and moreover I will give you a son by her; I will bless her, and she shall be a mother of nations; kings of peoples shall come from her" (Gn 17:15–16).

Motherhood is presented as a decisive gift of the Lord. The patriarch and his wife were given new names to indicate the unexpected and marvelous transformation that God would work in their life.

The visit of the three mysterious persons, whom the Fathers of the Church interpreted as a prefiguration of the Trinity, more explicitly announced the fulfillment of the promise to Abraham: "The Lord appeared to him by the oaks of Mamre, as he sat at the door of his tent in the heat of the day. He lifted up his eyes and looked, and behold, three men stood in front of him" (Gn 18:1–2). Abraham objected: "Shall a child be born to a man who is a hundred years old? Shall Sarah, who is ninety years old, bear a child?" (Gn 17:17; cf. 18:11–13). The divine guest replied: "Is anything too hard for the Lord? At the appointed time I will return to you, about this time next year, and Sarah shall have a son" (Gn 18:14; cf. Lk 1:37).

The narrative stresses the effect of the divine visit, which made fruitful a conjugal union that had been barren until then. Believing in the promise, Abraham became a father against all hope, and "father in the faith" because from his faith "descends" that of the Chosen People.

The Bible relates other stories of women released from sterility and gladdened by the Lord with the gift of motherhood. These are often situations of anguish, which God's intervention transforms into experiences of joy by receiving the heartfelt prayers of those who are humanly without hope. For example, "When Rachel saw that she bore Jacob no children, she envied her sister; and she said to Jacob, 'Give me children, or I shall die!' Jacob's anger was kindled against Rachel, and he said, 'Am I in the place of God, who has withheld from you the fruit of the womb?'" (Gn 30:1–2). But the biblical text immediately adds: "Then God remembered Rachel, and God hearkened to her and opened her womb. She conceived and bore a son" (Gn

30:22–23). This son, Joseph, would play a very important role for Israel at the time of the migration to Egypt.

In this as in other narratives, the Bible intends to highlight the marvelous nature of God's intervention in these specific cases by stressing the initial condition of the women's sterility. At the same time, however, it allows us to grasp the gratuitousness inherent in all motherhood.

We find a similar process in the account of the birth of Samson. The wife of Manoah, who had never been able to conceive a child, heard the Lord's announcement from the angel: "Behold, you are barren and have no children, but you shall conceive and bear a son" (Jgs 13:3). The unexpected and miraculous conception announced the great things that the Lord would do through Samson.

In the case of Hannah, Samuel's mother, the special role of prayer is underlined. Hannah suffered the humiliation of being barren but she was full of great trust in God, to whom she turned insistently, that he might help her to overcome this trial. One day at the temple she made a vow: "O Lord of hosts, if you will indeed look on the affliction of your maidservant and remember me, and not forget your maidservant, but will give to your maidservant a son, then I will give him to the Lord all the days of his life" (1 Sm 1:11).

Her prayer was answered: "The Lord remembered her," and "Hannah conceived and bore a son, and she called his name Samuel" (1 Sm 1:19–20). Keeping her promise, Hannah offered her son to the Lord: "For this child I prayed, and the Lord has granted me my petition which I made to him. Therefore, I have lent him to the Lord; as long as he lives, he is lent to the Lord" (1 Sm 1:27–28). Given by God to Hannah and then given by Hannah to God, the little Samuel became a living bond of communion between Hannah and God.

Samuel's birth was thus an experience of joy and an occasion for thanksgiving. The First Book of Samuel contains a

hymn known as Hannah's Magnificat, which seems to antici-
pate Mary's: "My heart exults in the Lord; my strength is
exalted in the Lord" (1 Sm 2:1). The grace of motherhood that
God granted to Hannah because of her ceaseless prayers filled
her with a new generosity. Samuel's consecration is the grateful response of a mother who, recognizing in her child the fruit
of God's mercy, returns his gift, entrusting to the Lord the child
she had so longed for.

In the accounts of miraculous motherhood which we have
recalled, it is easy to discover the important place the Bible
assigns to mothers in the mission of their sons. In Samuel's
case, Hannah had a determining role in deciding to give him to
the Lord. An equally decisive role was played by another
mother, Rebecca, who procured the inheritance for Jacob (cf.
Gn 27). That maternal intervention, described by the Bible, can
be interpreted as the sign of being chosen as an instrument in
God's sovereign plan. It was he who chose the youngest son,
Jacob, to receive the paternal blessing and inheritance, and
therefore to be the shepherd and leader of his people. It is God
who by a free and wise decision determines and governs each
one's destiny (Wis 10:10–12).

The Bible's message regarding motherhood reveals important and ever timely aspects. Indeed, it sheds light on the dimension of gratuitousness, which is apparent in the case of barren
women, God's particular covenant with woman, and the special bond between the destiny of the mother and that of the son.

At the same time, the intervention of God, who, at important moments in the history of his people, caused certain barren
women to conceive, prepared for belief in the intervention of
God who, in the fullness of time, would make a virgin fruitful
for the Incarnation of his Son.

General audience of March 6, 1996

Woman's Indispensable Role in Salvation History

The Old Testament holds up for our admiration some extraordinary women who, impelled by the Spirit of God, shared in the struggles and triumphs of Israel or contributed to its salvation. Their presence in the history of the people is neither marginal nor passive; they appear as true protagonists of salvation history. Here are the most significant examples.

After the crossing of the Red Sea, the sacred text emphasizes the initiative of a woman inspired to make this decisive event a festive celebration: "Then Miriam, the prophetess, the sister of Aaron, took a timbrel in her hand, and all the women went out after her with timbrels and dancing. And Miriam sang to them: 'Sing to the Lord, for he has triumphed gloriously; horse and rider he has thrown into the sea'" (Ex 15:20–21). This mention of feminine enterprise in the context of a celebration stresses not only the importance of woman's role, but also her particular ability for praising and thanking God.

The action of the prophetess Deborah at the time of the Judges is even more important. After ordering the commander of the army to go and gather his men, she guaranteed by her presence the success of Israel's army. She predicted that another woman, Jael, would kill their enemy's general.

To celebrate the great victory, Deborah also sang a long canticle praising Jael's action: "Most blessed of women be Jael...of tent-dwelling women most blessed" (Jgs 5:24). In the New Testament this praise is echoed in the words Elizabeth addressed to Mary on the day of the visitation: "Blessed are you among women..." (Lk 1:42).

The significant role of women in the salvation of their people, highlighted by the figures of Deborah and Jael, is presented again in the story of another prophetess named Huldah, who lived at the time of King Josiah. Questioned by the priest Hilkiah, she made prophecies announcing that forgiveness would be shown to the king who feared the divine wrath. Huldah thus became a messenger of mercy and peace (cf. 2 Kgs 22:14–20).

The Books of Judith and Esther, whose purpose is to idealize the positive contribution of woman to the history of the Chosen People, present—in a violent cultural context—two women who won victory and salvation for the Israelites. The Book of Judith, in particular, tells of a fearsome army sent by Nebuchadnezzar to conquer Israel. Led by Holofernes, the enemy army was ready to seize the city of Bethulia, amid the desperation of its inhabitants. Considering any resistance to be useless, they asked their rulers to surrender. But the city's elders, who in the absence of immediate aid declared themselves ready to hand Bethulia over to the enemy, were rebuked by Judith for their lack of faith as she professed her complete trust in the salvation that comes from the Lord.

After a long invocation to God, she who is a symbol of fidelity to the Lord, of humble prayer and of the intention to remain chaste, went to Holofernes, the proud, idolatrous and dissolute enemy general. Left alone with him and before striking him, Judith prayed to Yahweh, saying: "Give me strength this day, O Lord God of Israel!" (Jdt 13:7). Then, taking Holofernes' sword, she cut off his head.

Here too, as in the case of David and Goliath, the Lord used weakness to triumph over strength. On this occasion, however, a woman brought victory. Without being held back by the cowardice and unbelief of the people's rulers, Judith went to Holofernes and killed him, earning the gratitude and praise of the high priest and the elders of Jerusalem. The latter exclaimed to the woman who had defeated the enemy: "You are the exaltation of Jerusalem; you are the great glory of Israel; you are the great pride of our nation! You have done all this single-handedly; you have done great good to Israel, and God is well pleased with it. May the Almighty Lord bless you forever" (Jdt 15:9–10).

The events narrated in the Book of Esther occurred in another very difficult situation for the Jews. In the kingdom of Persia, Haman, the king's superintendent, decreed the extermination of the Jews. To remove the danger, Mordecai, a Jew living in the citadel of Susa, turned to his niece Esther, who lived in the king's palace where she had attained the rank of queen. Contrary to the law in force, she presented herself to the king without being summoned, thus risking the death penalty, and she obtained the revocation of the extermination decree. Haman was executed; Mordecai came to power and the Jews, delivered from menace, thus got the better of their enemies.

Judith and Esther both risked their lives to win the salvation of their people. The two interventions, however, were quite different. Esther did not kill the enemy but, by playing the role of mediator, interceded for those who were threatened with destruction.

The First Book of Samuel later attributed this intercessory role to another female figure, Abigail, the wife of Nabal. Here, too, it was due to her intervention that salvation was once again achieved. She went to meet David, who had decided to destroy Nabal's family, and asked forgiveness for her husband's sins. Thus, she delivered his house from certain destruction (1 Sm 25).

As can be easily noted, the Old Testament tradition frequently emphasizes the decisive action of women in the salvation of Israel, especially in the writings closest to the coming of Christ. In this way the Holy Spirit, through the events connected with Old Testament women, sketches with ever greater precision the characteristics of Mary's mission in the work of salvation for the entire human race.

General audience of March 27, 1996

The Ideal Woman Is a Precious Treasure

The Old Testament and the Judaic tradition are full of acknowledgments of woman's moral nobility. This is expressed above all in an attitude of trust in the Lord, in prayer to obtain the gift of motherhood and in imploring God for Israel's salvation from the assaults of its enemies. Sometimes, as in Judith's case, this quality was celebrated by the entire community, becoming the object of common admiration.

Beside the shining examples of the biblical heroines, the negative witnesses of some women are not lacking, such as Delilah who destroyed Samson's prophetic ability (Jgs 16:4–21); the foreign women who in Solomon's old age turned the king's heart away from the Lord and made him worship other gods (1 Kgs 11:1–8); Jezebel who killed all "the prophets of the Lord" (1 Kgs 18:13) and had Naboth killed, to give his vineyard to Ahab (1 Kgs 21); and Job's wife who insulted him in his misfortune and spurred him to rebel (Jb 2:9). In these cases, the woman's conduct was reminiscent of Eve's. However, the prevailing outlook in the Bible is that inspired by the Protogospel, which sees in woman an ally of God.

If foreign women were accused of turning Solomon away from his devotion to the true God, the Book of Ruth presents us instead with the most noble figure of a foreign woman: Ruth the

Moabite, an example of piety to her relatives and of sincere and generous humility. Sharing Israel's life and faith, she was to become David's great-grandmother and an ancestor of the Messiah. Inserting her in Jesus' genealogy (Mt 1:5), Matthew made her a sign of universality and a proclamation of God's mercy which extends to all humanity.

Among Jesus' forebears, the first evangelist also mentions Tamar, Rahab and Uriah's wife. These three sinful but not wicked women are listed among the female ancestors of the Messiah, in order to proclaim that divine goodness is greater than sin. Through his grace, God caused their irregular matrimonial situations to contribute to his plans of salvation, thereby also preparing for the future.

Another example of humble dedication, different from Ruth's, is represented by Jephthah's daughter. She agreed to pay for her father's victory over the Ammonites with her own death (Jgs 11:34–40). Lamenting her cruel destiny, she did not rebel but gave herself up to death in fulfillment of the thoughtless vow made by her parent in the context of primitive customs that were still prevalent (cf. Jer 7:31; Mi 6:6–8).

Although sapiential literature frequently alludes to woman's defects, it perceives in her a hidden treasure. "He who finds a wife finds a good thing, and obtains favor from the Lord" says the Book of Proverbs (18:22), expressing convinced appreciation of the feminine figure, a precious gift of the Lord.

At the end of the same book the portrait of the ideal woman is sketched. Far from representing an unattainable model, she is a concrete image born from the experience of women of great value: "Who can find a good wife? She is far more precious than jewels..." (Prov 31:10).

In this context, the Book of Maccabees holds up to us the most admirable example of nobility in trial, in the story of the seven brothers martyred during Antiochus Epiphanes' persecution. After describing the death of the seven brothers, the sacred author adds: "The mother was especially admirable and worthy of honorable memory. Though she saw her seven sons perish within a single day, she bore it with good courage because of her hope in the Lord. She encouraged each of them in the language of their fathers. Filled with a noble spirit, she fired her woman's reasoning with a man's courage," thus expressing her hope in a future resurrection. "Therefore the Creator of the world, who shaped the beginning of man and devised the origin of all things, will in his mercy give life and breath back to you again, since you now forget yourselves for the sake of his laws" (2 Mc 7:20–23).

Urging her seventh son to submit to death rather than disobey the divine law, the mother expressed her faith in the work of God who creates all things from nothing: "I beseech you, my child, to look at the heaven and the earth and see everything that is in them, and recognize that God did not make them out of things that existed. Thus also mankind comes into being. Do not fear this butcher, but prove worthy of your brothers" (2 Mc 7:28–29). She then gave herself up to a bloody death, after suffering torture of the heart seven times, witnessing to steadfast faith, boundless hope and heroic courage.

In these figures of woman, in whom the marvels of divine grace are manifest, we glimpse the one who will be the greatest: Mary, Mother of the Lord.

General audience of April 10, 1996

God Is Ever Faithful to His Covenant

The Bible often uses the expression "Daughter of Zion" to indicate the inhabitants of the city of Jerusalem, of which Mount Zion is historically and religiously the most significant (cf. Mi 4:10–13; Zep 3:14–18; Zec 2:14; 9:9–10). This feminine personalization facilitates the spousal interpretation of the loving relationship between God and Israel, frequently described with the terms "betrothed" or "wife."

Salvation history is the story of God's love, but often too of human infidelity. The Word of the Lord frequently reprimands the wife-people who break the marital covenant established with God: "Surely, as a faithless wife leaves her husband, so have you been faithless to me, O house of Israel" (Jer 3:20), and invites the children of Israel to plead with their mother: "Plead with your mother, plead—for she is not my wife, and I am not her husband" (Hos 2:2).

What is the sin of infidelity that stains Israel, Yahweh's "wife"? It consists above all in idolatry. According to the sacred text, in the Lord's eyes recourse to idols by his chosen people is equivalent to adultery.

With strong and dramatic images the prophet Hosea develops the theme of the spousal covenant between God and his people and of their betrayal. Hosea's personal experience becomes an eloquent symbol of it. Indeed, at the birth of his children he is ordered: "Call her name 'Not Pitied,' for I will no more have pity on the house of Israel, to forgive them at all," and again: "Call his name 'Not My People,' for you are not my people and I am not your God" (Hos 1:6, 9).

The Lord's rebuke and the disappointing experience of worshipping idols makes the faithless wife return to her senses. Repentant, she will say: "I will go and return to my first husband, for it was better with me then than now" (Hos 2:7). But God himself wishes to reestablish the covenant, and then his word becomes memory, mercy and tenderness: "Therefore, behold, I will allure her and bring her into the wilderness, and speak tenderly to her" (Hos 2:14). The wilderness is the place where God made his definitive covenant with his people after their deliverance from slavery.

Through these images of love, which portray the difficult relationship between God and Israel, the prophet illustrates the great tragedy of sin, the unhappiness of the way of infidelity and the efforts of divine love to speak to human hearts and bring them back to the covenant.

Despite the problems of the moment, through the mouth of the prophet God announces a more perfect covenant for the future: "And in that day, says the Lord, you will call me, 'my husband,' and no longer will you call me, 'my Baal'.... And I will betroth you to me forever; I will betroth you to me in righteousness and in justice, in steadfast love and in mercy. I will betroth you to me in faithfulness, and you shall know the Lord" (Hos 2:16, 19–20).

The Lord is not discouraged by human weakness but responds to human infidelities by proposing a more stable and intimate union: "I will sow him for myself in the land. And I will have pity on 'Not Pitied' and I will say to 'Not My People,' 'You are My People,' and he shall say, 'You are my God'" (Hos 2:23).

The same prospect of a new covenant is presented again by Jeremiah to the people in exile: "'At that time,' says the Lord, 'I will be the God of all the families of Israel, and they shall be my people.' Thus says the Lord: 'The people who survived the sword found grace in the wilderness; when Israel sought for rest, the Lord appeared to him from afar. I have loved you with an everlasting love; therefore, I have continued my faithfulness to you. Again I will build you, and you shall be built, O virgin Israel'" (Jer 31:1–4). Despite the people's infidelity, God's eternal love is always ready to reestablish the pact of love and to offer a salvation beyond all expectation.

Ezekiel and Isaiah also mention the image of the unfaithful woman who is forgiven. Through Ezekiel the Lord tells his wife: "Yet I will remember my covenant with you in the days of your youth, and I will establish with you an everlasting covenant" (Ez 16:60).

The Book of Isaiah quotes an oracle filled with tenderness: "For your Maker is your husband.... For a brief moment I forsook you, but with great compassion I will gather you. In overflowing wrath for a moment I hid my face from you, but with everlasting love I will have compassion on you, says the Lord, your redeemer" (Is 54:5, 7–8).

That promise to the Daughter of Zion is a new and faithful love, a magnificent hope which overcomes the abandonment of the faithless wife: "Say to the daughter Zion: 'Behold, your salvation comes; behold, his reward is with him, and his recompense before him.' And they shall be called the holy people, the redeemed of the Lord; and you shall be called 'Sought Out,' a city not forsaken" (Is 62:11–12).

The prophet explains: "You shall no more be termed 'Forsaken,' and your land shall no more be termed 'Desolate,' but you shall be called 'My Delight Is in Her,' and your land 'Married'; for the Lord delights in you and your land shall be married. For as a young man marries a virgin, your Builder shall marry you, and as the bridegroom rejoices over his bride, so shall your God rejoice over you" (Is 62:4–5).

These are images and attitudes of love, which the Canticle of Canticles summarizes in the statement: "I am my beloved's and my beloved is mine" (Sg 6:3). Thus the relationship between Yahweh and his people is presented again in ideal terms. When she listened to the reading of the prophecies, Mary must have thought of this perspective, which nourished messianic hope in her heart.

The rebukes addressed to the unfaithful people must have inspired in her a more ardent commitment of fidelity to the covenant, opening her spirit to the proposal of a definitive spousal communion with the Lord in grace and love. From this new covenant would come the salvation of the whole world.

General audience of April 24, 1996

Mary Responds
to God with Spousal Love

At the time of the annunciation, the angel greeted Mary, the "exalted Daughter of Zion" (*LG* 55), as the representative of humanity, called to give her own consent to the Incarnation of the Son of God. The first word the angel addressed to her was an invitation to joy: *chaïré,* that is, "rejoice." The Greek term has been translated in Latin with "Ave," a simple expression of greeting which does not seem to correspond fully to the divine messenger's intentions and the context in which the meeting takes place.

Of course, *chaïré* was also a form of greeting the Greeks frequently used, but the extraordinary circumstances in which it was uttered have nothing to do with the atmosphere of a habitual meeting. We must not forget that the angel is aware of bringing an announcement that is unique in human history; thus a simple, normal greeting would be out of place. Instead, the reference to the original meaning of the expression *chaïré,* which is "rejoice," seems more suitable for this exceptional occasion. As the Greek Fathers in particular constantly pointed out, citing various prophetic oracles, the invitation to joy is especially appropriate for the announcement of the Messiah's coming.

Our thoughts turn first of all to the prophet Zephaniah. The text of the annunciation shows a significant parallelism with his oracle: "Sing aloud, O daughter of Zion; shout, O Israel! Rejoice and exult with all your heart, O daughter of Jerusalem!" (Zep 3:14). There is the invitation to joy: "Rejoice and exult with all your heart" (v. 14). The Lord's presence is mentioned: "The king of Israel, the Lord, is in your midst" (v. 15). There is the exhortation not to be afraid: "Do not fear, O Zion; let not your hands grow weak" (v. 16). Finally, there is the promise of God's saving intervention: "The Lord your God is in your midst, a warrior who gives victory" (v. 17). The comparisons are so numerous and regular that they lead one to recognize Mary as the new Daughter of Zion, who has full reason to rejoice because God has decided to fulfill his plan of salvation.

A similar invitation to joy, even if it is in a different context, comes from Joel's prophecy: "Fear not, O land; be glad and rejoice, for the Lord has done great things!... You shall know that I am in the midst of Israel" (Jl 2:21–27).

The oracle of Zechariah is also significant; it is cited in connection with Jesus' entry into Jerusalem (Mt 21:5; Jn 12:15). In it the reason for joy is seen in the coming of the messianic king: "Rejoice greatly, O daughter of Zion! Shout aloud, O daughter of Jerusalem! Lo, your king comes to you; triumphant and victorious is he, humble...and he shall command peace to the nations" (Zec 9:9–10).

Finally, in the Book of Isaiah, the announcement of joy to the new Zion springs from its numerous posterity, a sign of divine blessing: "Sing, O barren one who did not bear; break forth into singing and cry aloud, you who have not been in travail! For the children of the desolate one will be more than the children of her that is married, says the Lord" (Is 54:1).

The three reasons for the invitation to joy—God's saving presence among his people, the coming of the messianic king, and gratuitous and superabundant fruitfulness—find their fulfillment in Mary. They justify the pregnant meaning which tradition attributes to the angel's greeting. By inviting her to assent to the fulfillment of the messianic promise and announcing to her the most high dignity of being Mother of the Lord, the angel could not but invite her to rejoice. Indeed, as the Council reminds us: "With her, the exalted Daughter of Zion, and after a long expectation of the promise, the times are fulfilled and the new economy established, when the Son of God took a human nature from her, that he might in the mysteries of his flesh free man from sin" (*LG* 55).

The account of the annunciation allows us to recognize in Mary the new Daughter of Zion, whom God invited to deep joy. It expresses her extraordinary role as mother of the Messiah, indeed as mother of the Son of God. The Virgin accepted the message on behalf of the people of David, but we can say that she accepted it on behalf of all humanity, because the Old Testament extended the role of the Davidic Messiah to all nations (cf. Ps 2:8; 72:8). In the divine intention, the announcement addressed to her looks to universal salvation.

To confirm this universal perspective of God's plan, we can recall several Old and New Testament texts which compare salvation to a great feast for all peoples on Mount Zion (cf. Is 25:6 ff.) and which announce the final banquet of God's kingdom (cf. Mt 22:1–10).

As Daughter of Zion, Mary is the virgin of the covenant which God establishes with all humanity. Mary's representational role in this event is clear, and it is significant that a woman carries out this function.

As the new Daughter of Zion, Mary was particularly suited to entering into the spousal covenant with God. More and better than any member of the Chosen People, she could offer the Lord the true heart of a bride. With Mary, "Daughter of Zion" is not merely a collective subject, but a person who represents humanity. At the moment of the annunciation, she responded to the proposal of divine love with her own spousal love. Thus she welcomed in a quite special way the joy foretold by the prophecies, a joy which reaches its peak here in the fulfillment of God's plan.

General audience of May 1, 1996

The Blessed Virgin
Was Filled with God's Grace

In the account of the annunciation, the first word of the angel's greeting, "rejoice," is an invitation to joy which recalls the oracles of the Old Testament addressed to the Daughter of Zion. We pointed this out in our previous catecheses and also explained the reasons for this invitation: God's presence among his people, the coming of the messianic king, and maternal fruitfulness. These reasons are fulfilled in Mary.

The angel Gabriel, addressing the Virgin of Nazareth after the greeting *chaïré,* "rejoice," calls her *kécharitôménê,* "full of grace." The words of the Greek text, *chaïré* and *kécharitôménê,* are deeply interconnected. Mary is invited to rejoice primarily because God loves her and has filled her with grace in view of her divine motherhood!

The Church's faith and the experience of the saints teach us that grace is a source of joy, and that true joy comes from God. In Mary, as in Christians, the divine gift produces deep joy.

Kécharitôménê: this term addressed to Mary seems to be the proper way to describe the woman destined to become the mother of Jesus. *Lumen Gentium* appropriately recalls this when it affirms: "The Virgin of Nazareth is greeted, on God's command, by an angel messenger as 'full of grace'" (*LG* 56). The fact that the heavenly messenger addresses her in this way enhances the value of the angelic greeting. It is a manifestation of God's mysterious saving plan in Mary's regard. As I wrote in the Encyclical *Redemptoris Mater:* "The 'fullness of grace' indicates all the supernatural munificence from which Mary benefits by being chosen and destined to be the Mother of Christ" (n. 9).

"Full of grace" is the name Mary possesses in the eyes of God. Indeed, according to Luke's account, the angel uses this expression even before he speaks the name "Mary," and thus emphasizes the predominant aspect which the Lord perceived in the Virgin of Nazareth's personality.

The expression "full of grace" is the translation of the Greek word *kécharitôménê,* which is a passive participle. Therefore, to render more exactly the nuance of the Greek word, one should not say merely "full of grace," but "made full of grace," or even "filled with grace," which would clearly indicate that this was a gift God gave to the Blessed Virgin. This term, in the form of a perfect participle, enhances the image of a perfect and lasting grace which implies fullness. The same verb, in the sense of "to bestow grace," is used in Ephesians to indicate the abundance of grace the Father granted to us in his beloved Son (Eph 1:6), and which Mary received as the first fruits of redemption (cf. *RM* 10).

In the Virgin's case, God's action certainly seems surprising. Mary has no human claim to receiving the announcement of the Messiah's coming. She is not the high priest, official representative of the Hebrew religion, nor even a man, but a young woman without any influence in the society of her time. In addition, she is a native of Nazareth, a village which is never mentioned in the Old Testament. It must not have enjoyed a good reputation, as Nathanael's question recorded in John's Gospel makes clear: "Can anything good come out of Nazareth?" (Jn 1:46).

The extraordinary and gratuitous nature of God's intervention becomes even clearer in comparison with Luke's text which recounts what happened to Zechariah. The latter's priestly status is highlighted as well as his exemplary life, which make him and his wife Elizabeth models of Old Testament righteousness. They walked "blameless in all the commandments and ordinances of the Lord" (Lk 1:6).

But we are not informed of Mary's origins either. The expression "of the house of David" (Lk 1:27) refers only to Joseph. No mention is made then of Mary's behavior. With this literary choice, Luke stresses that everything in Mary derives from a sovereign grace. All that is granted to her is not due to any claim of merit, but only to God's free and gratuitous choice.

In so doing, the evangelist does not of course intend to downplay the outstanding personal value of the Blessed Virgin. Rather, he wishes to present Mary as the pure fruit of God's goodwill. He has so taken possession of her as to make her, according to the title used by the angel, "full of grace." The abundance of grace itself is the basis of Mary's hidden spiritual richness.

In the Old Testament, Yahweh expresses the superabundance of his love in many ways and on many occasions. At the dawn of the New Testament, the gratuitousness of God's mercy reaches the highest degree in Mary. In her, God's predilection, shown to the Chosen People and in particular to the humble and the poor, reaches its culmination.

Nourished by the Word of the Lord and the experience of the saints, the Church urges believers to keep their gaze fixed on the Mother of the Redeemer and to consider themselves, like her, loved by God. She invites them to share our Lady's humility and poverty, so that, after her example and through her intercession, they may persevere in the grace of God who sanctifies and transforms hearts.

General audience of May 8, 1996

Mary Was Conceived Without Original Sin

Mary, "full of grace," has been recognized by the Church as "entirely holy and free from all stain of sin," "adorned from the first instant of her conception with the radiance of an entirely unique holiness" (*LG* 56). This recognition required a long process of doctrinal reflection, which finally led to the solemn proclamation of the dogma of the immaculate conception.

The title "made full of grace," which the angel addressed to Mary at the annunciation, refers to the exceptional divine favor shown to the young woman of Nazareth in view of the motherhood which was announced. But it indicates more directly the effect of divine grace in Mary; Mary was inwardly and permanently imbued with grace and thus sanctified. The title *kécharitôménê* has a very rich meaning and the Holy Spirit has never ceased deepening the Church's understanding of it.

In the preceding catechesis I pointed out that in the angel's greeting the expression "full of grace" serves almost as a name: it is Mary's name in the eyes of God. In Semitic usage, a name expresses the reality of the persons and things to which it refers. As a result, the title "full of grace" shows the deepest dimension of the young woman of Nazareth's personality: fashioned by grace and the object of divine favor to the point that she can be defined by this special predilection.

The Council recalls that the Church Fathers alluded to this truth when they called Mary the "all-holy one," affirming at the same time that she was "fashioned by the Holy Spirit and formed as a new creature" (*LG* 56). Grace, understood in the sense of "sanctifying grace" which produces personal holiness, brought about the new creation in Mary, making her fully conformed to God's plan.

Doctrinal reflection could thus attribute to Mary a perfection of holiness that, in order to be complete, had necessarily to include the beginning of her life. Bishop Theoteknos of Livias in Palestine, who lived between 550 and 650, seems to have moved in the direction of this original purity. In presenting Mary as "holy and all-fair," "pure and stainless," he referred to her birth in these words: "She is born like the cherubim, she who is a pure, immaculate clay" (*Panegyric for the Feast of the Assumption,* 5–6).

This last expression, recalling the creation of the first man, fashioned of a clay not stained by sin, attributes the same characteristics to Mary's birth. The Virgin's origin was also "pure and immaculate," that is, without any sin. The comparison with the cherubim also emphasizes the outstanding holiness that characterized Mary's life from the beginning of her existence.

Theoteknos' assertion marks a significant stage in the theological reflection on the mystery of the Lord's Mother. The Greek and Eastern Fathers had acknowledged a purification brought about by grace in Mary, either before the Incarnation (St. Gregory Nazianzen, *Oratio,* 38, 16) or at the very moment of the Incarnation (St. Ephrem, Severian of Gabala, James of Sarug). Theoteknos of Livias seems to have required of Mary an absolute purity from the beginning of her life. Indeed, she who was destined to become the Savior's Mother had to have had a perfectly holy, completely stainless origin.

In the eighth century, Andrew of Crete was the first theologian to see a new creation in Mary's birth. This is how he reasoned: "Today humanity, in all the radiance of her immaculate nobility, receives its ancient beauty. The shame of sin had darkened the splendor and attraction of human nature, but when the mother of the fair one *par excellence* is born, this nature regains in her person its ancient privileges and is fashioned according to a perfect model truly worthy of God.... The reform of our nature begins today and the aged world, subjected to a wholly divine transformation, receives the first fruits of the second creation" *(Sermon I on the Birth of Mary).*

Then, taking up again the image of the primordial clay, he states: "The Virgin's body is ground which God has tilled, the first fruits of Adam's soil divinized by Christ, the image truly like the former beauty, the clay kneaded by the divine artist" *(Sermon I on the Dormition of Mary).*

Mary's pure and immaculate conception is thus seen as the beginning of the new creation. It is a question of a personal privilege granted to the woman chosen to be Christ's Mother, who ushers in the time of abundant grace God willed for all humanity. This doctrine, taken up again in the eighth century by St. Germanus of Constantinople and St. John Damascene, sheds light on the value of Mary's original holiness, presented as the beginning of the world's redemption.

In this way the Church's tradition assimilates and makes explicit the authentic meaning of the title "full of grace" which the angel gave to the Blessed Virgin. Mary is full of sanctifying grace and was so from the first moment of her existence. This grace, according to Ephesians (1:6), is bestowed in Christ on all believers. Mary's original holiness represents the unsurpassable model of the gift and the distribution of Christ's grace in the world.

General audience of May 15, 1996

Mary's Enmity
toward Satan Was Absolute

As we saw in the preceding catecheses, since the sixth century the doctrinal reflection of the Eastern Church has interpreted the expression "full of grace" as a unique holiness which Mary enjoys throughout her existence. She thus initiates the new creation.

Along with Luke's account of the annunciation, tradition and the magisterium have seen in the so-called proto-evangelium (Gn 3:15) a scriptural source for the truth of Mary's immaculate conception. On the basis of the ancient Latin version: "She will crush your head," this text inspired many depictions of the Immaculata crushing the serpent under her feet.

On an early occasion we recalled that this version does not agree with the Hebrew text, in which it is not the woman but her offspring, her descendant, who will bruise the serpent's head. This text then does not attribute the victory over Satan to Mary but to her Son. Nevertheless, since the biblical concept establishes a profound solidarity between the parent and the offspring, the depiction of the Immaculata crushing the serpent, not by her own power but through the grace of her Son, is consistent with the original meaning of the passage.

The same biblical text also proclaims the enmity between the woman and her offspring on the one hand and the serpent and his offspring on the other. This is a hostility expressly established by God, which has a unique importance, if we consider the problem of the Virgin's personal holiness. In order to be the irreconcilable enemy of the serpent and his offspring, Mary had to be free from all power of sin, and to be so from the first moment of her existence.

In this regard, the Encyclical *Fulgens Corona,* published by Pope Pius XII in 1953 to commemorate the centenary of the definition of the dogma of the immaculate conception, reasons thus: "If at a given moment the Blessed Virgin Mary had been left without divine grace, because she was defiled at her conception by the hereditary stain of sin, between her and the serpent there would no longer have been—at least during this period of time, however brief—that eternal enmity spoken of in the earliest tradition up to the definition of the immaculate conception, but rather a certain enslavement" (*AAS* 45 [1953], 579).

The absolute hostility put between the woman and the devil thus demands in Mary the immaculate conception, that is, a total absence of sin, from the beginning of her life. The Son of Mary won the definitive victory over Satan and enabled his Mother to receive its benefits in advance by preserving her from sin. As a result, the Son granted her the power to resist the devil, thus achieving in the mystery of the immaculate conception the most notable effect of his redeeming work.

By drawing our attention to Mary's special holiness and her complete removal from Satan's influence, the title "full of grace" and the proto-evangelium enables us to perceive in the unique privilege the Lord granted to Mary the beginning of a new order. It is the result of friendship with God and, as a consequence, entails a profound enmity between the serpent and men.

The 12th chapter of Revelation, which speaks of the "woman clothed with the sun," (12:1), is often cited too as biblical testimony on behalf of the immaculate conception. Current exegesis agrees in seeing in this woman the community of God's People, giving birth in pain to the risen Messiah. Along with the collective interpretation, however, the text suggests an individual one in the statement: "She brought forth a male child, one who is to rule all the nations with a rod of iron" (12:5). With this reference to childbirth, it is acknowledged that the woman clothed with the sun is in a certain sense identified with Mary, the woman who gave birth to the Messiah. The woman-community is actually described with the features of the woman-Mother of Jesus.

Identified by her motherhood, the woman "was with child and she cried out in her pangs of birth, in anguish for her delivery" (12:2). This note refers to the Mother of Jesus at the cross (cf. Jn 19:25). There, with a soul pierced by the sword, she shared in anguish for the delivery of the community of disciples (cf. Lk 2:35). Despite her sufferings, she is "clothed with the sun"—that is, she reflects the divine splendor—and appears as a "great sign" of God's spousal relationship with his people. Although not directly indicating the privilege of the immaculate conception, these images can be interpreted as an expression of the Father's loving care which surrounds Mary with the grace of Christ and the splendor of the Spirit.

Finally, the Book of Revelation invites us more particularly to recognize the ecclesial dimension of Mary's personality. The woman clothed with the sun represents the Church's holiness, which is fully realized in the holy Virgin by virtue of a singular grace.

These scriptural assertions, to which tradition and the magisterium refer in order to ground the doctrine of the immaculate conception, would seem to contradict the biblical texts which affirm the universality of sin. The Old Testament speaks of a sinful contamination which affects everyone "born of woman" (Ps 51:7; Jb 14:2).

In the New Testament, Paul states that, as a result of Adam's sin, "all men sinned," and that "one man's trespass led to condemnation for all men" (Rom 5:12, 18). Therefore, as the *Catechism of the Catholic Church* recalls, original sin "affected human nature," which is thus found "in a fallen state." Sin is therefore transmitted "by propagation to all mankind, that is, by the transmission of a human nature deprived of original holiness and justice" (n. 404). However, Paul admits an exception to this universal law: Christ, "who knew no sin" (2 Cor 5:21), was thus able "where sin increased" (Rom 5:20) to make grace abound all the more.

These assertions do not necessarily lead to the conclusion that Mary was involved in sinful humanity. The parallel Paul established between Adam and Christ is completed by that between Eve and Mary. The role of woman, important in the drama of sin, is equally so in the redemption of mankind.

St. Irenaeus presents Mary as the New Eve, who by her faith and obedience compensated for the disbelief and disobedience of Eve. Such a role in the economy of salvation requires the absence of sin. It was fitting that like Christ, the new Adam, Mary too, the New Eve, did not know sin and was thus capable of cooperating in the redemption.

Sin, which washes over humanity like a torrent, halts before the Redeemer and his faithful collaborator, but with a substantial difference: Christ is all holy by virtue of the grace that in his humanity derives from the divine person; Mary is all holy by virtue of the grace received by the merits of the Savior.

General audience of May 29, 1996

Christ's Grace
Preserved Mary from Sin

The doctrine of Mary's perfect holiness from the first moment of her conception met with a certain resistance in the West. This was on account of St. Paul's statements about original sin and the universality of sin, which St. Augustine took up again and explained with particular force.

This great doctor of the Church certainly realized that Mary's status as Mother of a completely holy Son required total purity and an extraordinary holiness. This is why in the controversy with Pelagius, Augustine stressed that Mary's holiness is an exceptional gift of grace, and stated in this regard: "We make an exception for the Blessed Virgin Mary, whom, for the sake of the Lord's honor, I would in no way like to be mentioned in connection with sin. Do we not know why she was granted a greater grace in view of the complete victory over sin, she who merited to conceive and give birth to him who obviously had no sin?" (*De natura et gratia,* n. 42).

Augustine stressed Mary's perfect holiness and the absence of any personal sin in her because of her lofty dignity as Mother of the Lord. Nonetheless, he could not understand how the affirmation of a total absence of sin at the time of conception could be reconciled with the doctrine of the universality of original sin and the need of redemption for all Adam's descendants. This conclusion was later reached by an ever more penetrating understanding of the Church's faith, explaining how Mary had benefited from Christ's redemptive grace from her conception.

In the ninth century the feast of Mary's conception was also introduced in the West, first in southern Italy, in Naples and then in England.

Around 1128, a monk of Canterbury, Eadmer, writing the first treatise on the immaculate conception, complained that its respective liturgical celebration, especially pleasing to those "in whom a pure simplicity and most humble devotion to God was found" (*Tract. de Conc. B.V.M.,* 1–2), had been set aside or suppressed. Wishing to promote the restoration of this feast, the devout monk rejected St. Augustine's objections to the privilege of the immaculate conception, based on the doctrine of the transmission of original sin in human generation. He fittingly employed the image of a chestnut "which is conceived, nourished and formed beneath its bur and yet is protected from being pricked by it" (*Tract.* 10). Even beneath the bur of an act of generation which in itself must transmit original sin, Eadmer argued, Mary was preserved from every stain by the explicit will of God. He "was obviously able to do this and wanted to do so. Thus, if he willed it, he did it" (*Tract.* 10).

Despite Eadmer, the great theologians of the 13th century made St. Augustine's difficulties their own, advancing this argument: the redemption accomplished by Christ would not be universal if the condition of sin were not common to all human beings. If Mary had not contracted original sin, she could not have been redeemed. Redemption consists in freeing those who are in the state of sin.

Following several 12th century theologians, Duns Scotus found the key to overcoming these objections to the doctrine of Mary's immaculate conception. He held that Christ, the perfect Mediator, exercised the highest act of mediation precisely in Mary by preserving her from original sin. Thus, he introduced into theology the concept of redemption by preservation. According to it, Mary was redeemed in an even more wonderful way, not by being freed from sin, but by being preserved from sin.

The insight of Bl. Duns Scotus, who later became known as "the Doctor of the Immaculata," was well received by theologians, especially Franciscans, from the beginning of the 14th century. After Sixtus IV's approval in 1477 of the Mass of the Conception, this doctrine was increasingly accepted in the theological schools.

This providential development of liturgy and doctrine prepared for the definition of the Marian privilege by the supreme magisterium. The latter only occurred many centuries later, and was spurred by a fundamental insight of faith: the Mother of Christ had to be perfectly holy from the very beginning of her life.

No one fails to see how the affirmation of the exceptional privilege granted to Mary stresses that Christ's redeeming action does not only free us from sin, but also preserves us from it. This dimension of preservation, which in Mary is total, is present in the redemptive intervention by which Christ, in freeing man from sin, also gives him the grace and strength to conquer its influence in his life.

In this way the dogma of Mary's immaculate conception does not obscure but rather helps wonderfully to shed light on the effects in human nature of Christ's redemptive grace.

Christians look to Mary, the first to be redeemed by Christ and who had the privilege of not being subjected even for an instant to the power of evil and sin, as the perfect model and icon of that holiness (cf. *LG* 65) which they are called to attain in their life, with the help of the Lord's grace.

General audience of June 5, 1996

Pius IX Defined the Immaculate Conception

Down the centuries, the conviction that Mary was pre-served from every stain of sin from her conception, so that she is to be called all holy, gradually gained ground in the liturgy and theology. At the start of the 19th century, this development led to a petition drive for a dogmatic definition of the privilege of the immaculate conception.

Around the middle of the century, with the intention of accepting this request, Pope Pius IX, after consulting the theo-logians, questioned the bishops about the opportuneness and the possibility of such a definition, convoking as it were a "council in writing." The result was significant: the vast major-ity of the 604 bishops gave a positive response to the question.

After such an extensive consultation, which emphasized my venerable Predecessor's concern to express the Church's faith in the definition of the dogma, he set about preparing the document with equal care.

The special commission of theologians which Pius IX set up to determine the revealed doctrine assigned the essential role to ecclesial practice. This criterion influenced the formula-tion of the dogma, which preferred expressions taken from the Church's lived experience, from the faith and worship of the Christian people, to scholastic definitions.

Finally in 1854, with the Bull *Ineffabilis,* Pius IX solemnly proclaimed the dogma of the immaculate conception: "We declare, pronounce and define that the doctrine which asserts that the Blessed Virgin Mary, from the first moment of her conception, by a singular grace and privilege of almighty God and in view of the merits of Jesus Christ, Savior of the human race, was preserved free from every stain of original sin is a doctrine revealed by God and, for this reason, must be firmly and constantly believed by all the faithful" (*DS* 2803).

The proclamation of the dogma of the immaculate conception expresses the essential datum of faith. Pope Alexander VII, in the Bull *Sollicitudo* of 1661, spoke of the preservation of Mary's soul "in its creation and infusion into the body" (*DS* 2017). Pius IX's definition, however, prescinds from all explanations about how the soul is infused into the body and attributes to the person of Mary, at the first moment of her conception, the fact of her being preserved from every stain of original sin.

The freedom "from every stain of original sin" entails as a positive consequence the total freedom from all sin as well as the proclamation of Mary's perfect holiness, a doctrine to which the dogmatic definition makes a fundamental contribution. The negative formulation of the Marian privilege, which resulted from the earlier controversies about original sin that arose in the West, must always be complemented by the positive expression of Mary's holiness more explicitly stressed in the Eastern tradition. Pius IX's definition refers only to the freedom from original sin and does not explicitly include freedom from concupiscence. Nevertheless, Mary's complete preservation from every stain of sin also has as a consequence her freedom from concupiscence, a disordered tendency which, according to the Council of Trent, comes from sin and inclines to sin (*DS* 1515)

Granted "by a singular grace and privilege of almighty God," this preservation from original sin is an absolutely gratuitous divine favor, which Mary received at the first moment of her existence. The dogmatic definition does not say that this singular privilege is unique, but lets that be intuited. The affirmation of this uniqueness, however, is explicitly stated in the Encyclical *Fulgens Corona* of 1953, where Pope Pius XII speaks of "the very singular privilege which was never granted to another person" (*AAS* 45 [1953], 580), thus excluding the possibility, maintained by some but without foundation, of attributing this privilege also to St. Joseph.

The virgin Mother received the singular grace of being immaculately conceived "in view of the merits of Jesus Christ, Savior of the human race," that is, of his universal redeeming action. The text of the dogmatic definition does not expressly declare that Mary was redeemed, but the Bull *Ineffabilis* states elsewhere that "she was redeemed in the most sublime way." This is the extraordinary truth: Christ was the Redeemer of his Mother and carried out his redemptive action in her "in the most perfect way" (*Fulgens Corona, AAS* 45 [1953], 581) from the first moment of her existence. The Second Vatican Council proclaimed that the Church "admires and exalts in Mary the most excellent fruit of the redemption" (*SC* 103).

This solemnly proclaimed doctrine is expressly termed a "doctrine revealed by God." Pope Pius IX adds that it must be "firmly and constantly believed by all the faithful." Consequently, whoever does not make this doctrine his own, or maintains an opinion contrary to it, "is shipwrecked in faith" and "separates himself from Catholic unity."

In proclaiming the truth of this dogma of the immaculate conception, my venerable Predecessor was conscious of exercising his power of infallible teaching as the universal pastor of the Church, which several years later would be solemnly defined at the First Vatican Council. Thus, he put his infallible magisterium into action as a service to the faith of God's People, and it is significant that he did so by defining Mary's privilege.

General audience of June 12, 1996

Mary Was Free from All Personal Sin

The definition of the dogma of the immaculate conception directly concerns only the first moment of Mary's existence, when she was "preserved free from every stain of original sin." The papal magisterium thus wished to define only the truth which had been the subject of controversy down the centuries—her preservation from original sin—and was not concerned with defining the lasting holiness of the Lord's virgin Mother. This truth already belongs to the common awareness of the Christian people. It testifies that Mary, free from original sin, was also preserved from all actual sin and that this initial holiness was granted to her in order to fill her entire life.

The Church has constantly regarded Mary as holy and free from all sin or moral imperfection. The Council of Trent expressed this conviction, affirming that no one "can avoid all sins, even venial sins, throughout his life, unless he is given a special privilege, as the Church holds with regard to the Blessed Virgin" (*DS* 1573). Even the Christian transformed and renewed by grace is not spared the possibility of sinning. Grace does not preserve him from all sin throughout his whole life, unless, as the Council of Trent asserts, a special privilege guarantees this immunity from sin. This is what happened with Mary.

The Council of Trent did not wish to define this privilege but stated that the Church vigorously affirms it: *tenet,* that is, she firmly holds it. This is a decision which, far from relegating this truth to pious belief or devotional opinion, confirms its nature as a solid doctrine, quite present in the faith of the People of God. Moreover, this conviction is based on the grace attributed to Mary by the angel at the time of the annunciation. Calling her "full of grace," *kécharitôménê,* the angel acknowledged her as the woman endowed with a lasting perfection and a fullness of sanctity, without shadow of sin or of moral or spiritual imperfection.

Several early Fathers of the Church, who were not yet convinced of her perfect holiness, attributed imperfections or moral defects to Mary. Some recent authors have taken the same position. However, the Gospel texts cited to justify these opinions provide no basis at all for attributing a sin or even a moral imperfection to the Mother of the Redeemer. The twelve-year-old Jesus' reply to his mother: "How is it that you sought me? Did you not know that I must be in my Father's house?" (Lk 2:49), has sometimes been interpreted as a veiled rebuke. A careful reading of the episode, however, shows that Jesus did not rebuke his Mother and Joseph for seeking him, since they were responsible for looking after him.

Coming upon Jesus after an anxious search, Mary asked him only the "why" of his behavior: "Son, why have you treated us so?" (Lk 2:48). Jesus answered with another "why," refraining from any rebuke and referring to the mystery of his divine sonship. Nor can the words he spoke at Cana: "O woman, what have you to do with me? My hour has not yet come" (Jn 2:4), be interpreted as a rebuke. Seeing the likely inconvenience which the lack of wine would have caused the bride and groom, Mary spoke to Jesus with simplicity, entrusting the problem to him. Though aware of being the Messiah bound to obey the Father's will alone, he answered his Mother's implicit request. He responded above all to the Virgin's faith and thus performed the first of his miracles, thereby manifesting his glory.

Later some gave a negative interpretation to the statement Jesus made at the beginning of his public life, when Mary and his relatives asked to see him. Relating to us Jesus' reply to the one who said to him: "Your mother and your brethren are standing outside, desiring to see you," the Evangelist Luke offers us the interpretive key to the account, which must be understood on the basis of Mary's inclinations. These were quite different from those of his "brethren" (cf. Jn 7:5). Jesus replied: "My mother and my brethren are those who hear the word of God and do it" (Lk 8:21). In the annunciation account, Luke shows how Mary is the model of listening to the Word of God and of generous docility. Interpreted in this perspective, the episode offers great praise of Mary, who perfectly fulfilled the divine plan in her own life. Although Jesus' words were opposed to the brethren's attempt, they exalt Mary's fidelity to the will of God and the greatness of her motherhood, which she lived not only physically but also spiritually.

In expressing this indirect praise, Jesus used a particular method: he stressed the nobility of Mary's conduct in the light of more general statements and showed more clearly the Virgin's solidarity with and closeness to humanity on the difficult way of holiness.

Lastly, the words: "Blessed rather are those who hear the Word of God and keep it!" (Lk 11:28), which Jesus spoke in reply to the woman who had called his Mother blessed, far from putting into doubt Mary's personal perfection, bring out her faithful fulfillment of the Word of God. So has the Church understood them, putting this sentence into the liturgical celebrations in Mary's honor. The Gospel text actually suggests that he made this statement to reveal that the highest reason for his Mother's blessedness lies precisely in her intimate union with God and her perfect submission to the divine Word.

The special privilege God granted to Mary who is "all holy" leads us to admire the marvels grace accomplished in her life. It also reminds us that Mary belonged always and completely to the Lord, and that no imperfection harmed her perfect harmony with God. Her earthly life was therefore marked by a constant, sublime growth in faith, hope and charity. For believers, Mary is thus the radiant sign of divine mercy and the sure guide to the loftiest heights of holiness and Gospel perfection.

General audience of June 19, 1996

Mary Freely Cooperated in God's Plan

In the Gospel account of the visitation, Elizabeth, "filled with the Holy Spirit," welcomed Mary to her home and exclaimed: "Blessed is she who believed that there would be a fulfillment of what was spoken to her from the Lord" (Lk 1:45). This beatitude, the first reported in Luke's Gospel, presents Mary as the one who, by her faith, precedes the Church in fulfilling the spirit of the beatitudes.

Elizabeth's praise of Mary's faith is reinforced by comparing it to the angel's announcement to Zechariah. A superficial reading of the two announcements might consider Zechariah and Mary as having given similar responses to the divine message: "How shall I know this? For I am an old man, and my wife is advanced in years," Zechariah said; and Mary: "How can this be since I have no husband?" (Lk 1:18, 34). But the profound difference between the interior attitudes of the principals in these two episodes can be seen from the words of the angel, who rebuked Zechariah for his disbelief, while he immediately replied to Mary's question. Unlike Elizabeth's husband, Mary fully submitted to the divine plan and did not condition her consent on the granting of a visible sign.

Mary reminded the angel, who proposed that she become a mother, of her intention to remain a virgin. Believing that the announcement could be fulfilled, she questioned the divine messenger only about the manner of its accomplishment. This was to better fulfill God's will, to which she intended to submit with total readiness. "She sought the manner; she did not doubt God's omnipotence," St. Augustine remarks *(Sermon 291).*

The context in which the two announcements are made also helps to exalt the excellence of Mary's faith. In Luke's account, we see the more favorable situation of Zechariah and the inadequacy of his response. He received the angel's announcement in the Temple of Jerusalem, at the altar before the "Holy of Holies" (cf. Ex 30:6–8). The angel addressed him as he was offering incense, thus, as he was carrying out his priestly duties, at a significant moment in his life. The divine decision was communicated to him in a vision. These particular circumstances favor an easier understanding of the divine authenticity of the message and offer an incentive to accept it promptly.

The announcement to Mary, however, took place in a simpler, workaday context, without the external elements of sacredness which accompanied the one made to Zechariah. Luke does not indicate the precise place where the annunciation of the Lord's birth occurred. Luke reports only that Mary was in Nazareth, a village of little importance, which did not seem predestined for the event. In addition, the evangelist does not ascribe unusual importance to the moment when the angel appears and does not describe the historical circumstances. In meeting the heavenly messenger, one's attention is focused on the meaning of his words, which demand of Mary intense listening and a pure faith.

This last consideration allows us to appreciate the greatness of Mary's faith especially in comparison with the tendency, then as now, to ask insistently for sensible signs in order to believe. In contrast, the Virgin's assent to the divine will was motivated only by her love of God.

Mary was asked to assent to a much loftier truth than that announced to Zechariah. The latter was invited to believe in a wondrous birth that would take place within a sterile marital union which God wished to make fruitful. It was a divine intervention similar to those benefiting several Old Testament women: Sarah (cf. Gn 17:15–21; 18:10–14), Rachel (cf. Gn 30:22), the mother of Samson (cf. Jgs 13:1–7), Hannah, the mother of Samuel (cf. 1 Sm 1: 11–20). In these episodes the gratuitousness of God's gift is especially emphasized.

Mary was called to believe in a virginal motherhood, for which the Old Testament mentions no precedent. The well-known prophecy of Isaiah: "Behold, a young woman shall conceive and bear a son, and shall call his name Emmanuel" (7:14), although not excluding such a view, was explicitly interpreted in this sense only after Christ's coming and in the light of the Gospel revelation.

Mary was asked to assent to a truth never expressed before. She accepted it with a simple yet daring heart. With the question: "How can this be?" she expressed her faith in the divine power to make virginity compatible with her exceptional and unique motherhood. By replying: "The Holy Spirit will come upon you, and the power of the Most High will overshadow you" (Lk 1:35), the angel offered God's ineffable solution to the question Mary asked. Virginity, which seemed an obstacle, became the concrete context in which the Holy Spirit would accomplish in her the conception of the incarnate Son of God. The angel's response opened the way to the Virgin's cooperation with the Holy Spirit in the begetting of Jesus. The free cooperation of the human person is realized in carrying out the divine plan. By believing in the Lord's word, Mary cooperated in fulfilling the motherhood announced to her.

The Fathers of the Church often stressed this aspect of Jesus' virginal conception. In commenting on the Gospel of the annunciation, St. Augustine in particular stated: "The angel announces; the Virgin listens, believes and conceives" *(Sermon 13 in Nat. Dom.)*. Again: "Christ is believed and conceived through faith. The coming of faith first occurs in the Virgin's heart and then fruitfulness comes to the Mother's womb *(Sermon 293)*.

Mary's act of faith recalls the faith of Abraham, who at the dawn of the Old Covenant, believed in God and thus became the father of a great posterity (cf. Gn 15:6; *RM* 14). At the start of the New Covenant, Mary also exerted with her faith a decisive influence on the fulfillment of the mystery of the Incarnation, the beginning and the synthesis of Jesus' entire redeeming mission. The close relationship between faith and salvation, which Jesus stressed in his public life (cf. Mt 5:34; 10:52; etc.), helps us also to understand the fundamental role which Mary's faith exercised and continues to exercise in the salvation of the human race.

General audience of July 3, 1996

The Virginal Conception
Is a Biological Fact

The Church has constantly held that Mary's virginity is a truth of faith, as the Church has received and reflected on the witness of the Gospels of Luke, of Matthew and probably also of John. In the episode of the annunciation, the evangelist Luke calls Mary a "virgin," referring both to her intention to persevere in virginity, as well as to the divine plan which reconciled this intention with her miraculous motherhood. The affirmation of the virginal conception, due to the action of the Holy Spirit, excludes every hypothesis of natural parthenogenesis and rejects the attempts to explain Luke's account as the development of a Jewish theme or as the derivation of a pagan mythological legend.

The structure of the Lucan text resists any reductive interpretation (cf. Lk 1:26–38; 2:19, 51). Its coherence does not validly support any mutilation of the terms or expressions which affirm the virginal conception brought about by the Holy Spirit.

Reporting the angel's announcement to Joseph, the Evangelist Matthew affirms like Luke that the conception was "the work of the Holy Spirit" (Mt 1:20) and excluded marital relations. Furthermore, Jesus' virginal conception was communicated to Joseph at a later time. For him it was not a question of being invited to give his assent prior to the conception of Mary's Son, the fruit of the supernatural intervention of the Holy Spirit and the cooperation of the mother alone. Joseph was merely asked to accept freely his role as the Virgin's husband and his paternal mission with regard to the child.

Matthew presents the virginal origins of Jesus as the fulfillment of Isaiah's prophecy. "'Behold, a virgin shall conceive and bear a son, and his name shall be called Emmanuel' (which means, 'God with us')" (Mt 1:23; cf. Is 7:14). In this way Matthew leads us to conclude that the virginal conception was the object of reflection in the first Christian community, which understood its conformity to the divine plan of salvation and its connection with the identity of Jesus, "God with us."

Unlike Luke and Matthew, Mark's Gospel does not mention Jesus' conception and birth. Nonetheless, it is worth noting that Mark never mentions Joseph, Mary's husband. Jesus is called "the son of Mary" by the people of Nazareth or in another context, and "the Son of God" several times (3:11; 5:7; cf. 1:11; 9:7; 14:61–62; 15:39). These facts are in harmony with belief in the mystery of his virginal conception. This truth, according to a recent exegetical discovery, would be explicitly contained in verse 13 of the Prologue of John's Gospel, which some ancient authoritative authors (for example, Irenaeus and Tertullian) present, not in the usual plural form, but in the singular: "He, who was born not of blood nor of the will of the flesh nor of the will of man, but of God." This version in the singular would make the Johannine Prologue one of the major attestations of Jesus' virginal conception, placed in the context of the mystery of the Incarnation.

Paul's paradoxical affirmation: "But when the time had fully come, God sent forth his Son, born of woman...so that we might receive adoption as sons" (Gal 4:4–5), paves the way to the question about this Son's personhood, and thus about his virginal birth.

The uniform Gospel witness testifies how faith in the virginal conception of Jesus was firmly rooted in various milieus of the early Church. This deprives of any foundation several recent interpretations which understand the virginal conception not in a physical or biological sense, but only as symbolic or metaphorical: it would designate Jesus as God's gift to humanity. The same can be said for the opinion advanced by others, that the account of the virginal conception would instead be a theologoumenon, that is, a way of expressing a theological doctrine, that of Jesus' divine sonship, or would be a mythological portrayal of him.

As we have seen, the Gospels contain the explicit affirmation of a virginal conception of the biological order, brought about by the Holy Spirit. The Church made this truth her own, beginning with the very first formulations of the faith (cf. *CCC* 496).

The faith expressed in the Gospels is confirmed without interruption in later tradition. The formulas of faith of the first Christian writers presuppose the assertion of the virginal birth. Aristides, Justin, Irenaeus and Tertullian agree with Ignatius of Antioch, who proclaimed Jesus "truly born of a virgin" (*Smyrn.* 1, 2). These authors mean a real, historical virginal conception of Jesus and are far from affirming a virginity that is only moral or a vague gift of grace manifested in the child's birth.

The solemn definitions of faith by the ecumenical councils and the papal magisterium, which follow the first brief formulas of faith, are in perfect harmony with this truth. The Council of Chalcedon (451), in its profession of faith, carefully phrased and with its infallibly defined content, affirmed that Christ was "begotten...as to his humanity in these last days, for us and for our salvation by the Virgin Mary, the Mother of God" (*DS* 301). In the same way the Third Council of Constantinople (681) proclaimed that Jesus Christ was "begotten...as to his humanity by the Holy Spirit and the Virgin Mary, she who is properly and in all truth the Mother of God" (*DS* 555). Other ecumenical councils (Constantinople II, Lateran IV and Lyons II) declared Mary "ever-virgin," stressing her perpetual virginity (*DS* 423, 801, 852). The Second Vatican Council took up these affirmations, highlighting the fact that Mary "by her belief and obedience, not knowing man but overshadowed by the Holy Spirit...brought forth on earth the very Son of the Father" (*LG* 63).

In addition to the conciliar definitions, there are the definitions of the papal Magisterium concerning the immaculate conception of the "Blessed Virgin Mary" (*DS* 2803) and the assumption of the "immaculate and ever-virgin Mother of God" (*DS* 3903).

Although the definitions of the magisterium, except for those of the Lateran Council of 649, desired by Pope Martin I, do not explain the meaning of the term "virgin," it is clear that this term is used in its customary sense: the voluntary abstention from sexual acts and the preservation of bodily integrity. However, physical integrity is considered essential to the truth of faith of Jesus' virginal conception (cf. *CCC* 496).

The description of Mary as "holy ever-virgin, immaculate" draws attention to the connection between holiness and virginity. Mary wanted a virginal life because she was motivated by the desire to give her whole heart to God. The expression used in the definition of the assumption, "the immaculate ever-virgin Mother of God," also implies the connection between Mary's virginity and her motherhood: two prerogatives miraculously combined in the conception of Jesus, true God and true man. Thus, Mary's virginity is intimately linked to her divine motherhood and perfect holiness.

General audience of July 10, 1996

Our Lady Intended to Remain a Virgin

Mary questioned the angel who told her of Jesus' conception and birth: "How can this be since I do not know man?" (Lk 1:34). Such a query seems surprising, to say the least, if we call to mind the biblical accounts that relate the announcement of an extraordinary birth to a childless woman. Those cases concerned married women who were naturally sterile, to whom God gave the gift of a child through their normal conjugal life (1 Sm 1:19–20), in response to their anguished prayers (cf. Gn 15:2; 30:22–23; 1 Sm 1:10; Lk 1:13).

Mary received the angel's message in a different situation. She was not a married woman with problems of sterility; by a voluntary choice she intended to remain a virgin. Therefore, her intention of virginity, the fruit of her love for the Lord, appeared to be an obstacle to the motherhood announced to her.

At first sight, Mary's words would seem merely to express only her present state of virginity: Mary would affirm that she does not "know" man, that is, that she is a virgin. Nevertheless, the context in which the question was asked: "How can this be?" and the affirmation that follows: "since I do not know man," emphasize both Mary's present virginity and her intention to remain a virgin. The expression she used, with the verb in the present tense, reveals the permanence and continuity of her state.

Mentioning this difficulty, Mary did not at all oppose the divine plan, but showed her intention to conform totally to it. Moreover, the girl from Nazareth always lived in full harmony with the divine will and had chosen a virginal life with the intention of pleasing the Lord. Her intention of virginity disposed her to accept God's will "with all her human and feminine 'I,' and this response of faith included both perfect cooperation with the 'grace of God that precedes and assists' and perfect openness to the action of the Holy Spirit" (*RM* 13).

To some, Mary's words and intentions appear improbable, since in the Jewish world virginity was considered neither a value nor an ideal to be pursued. The same Old Testament writings confirm this in several well-known episodes and expressions. In the Book of Judges, for example, Jephthah's daughter who, having to face death while still young and unmarried, bewailed her virginity, that is, she lamented that she had been unable to marry (Jgs 11:38). Marriage, moreover, by virtue of the divine command, "Be fruitful and multiply" (Gn 1:28), was considered woman's natural vocation which involves the joys and sufferings that go with motherhood.

In order to understand better the context in which Mary's decision came to maturity, it is necessary to remember that in the period immediately preceding the beginning of the Christian era, a certain positive attitude to virginity began to appear in some Jewish circles. For example, the Essenes, of whom many important historical testimonies have been found at Qumran, lived in celibacy or restricted the use of marriage because of community life and the search for greater intimacy with God.

Furthermore, in Egypt there was a community of women who, associated with the Essene spirituality, observed continence. These women, the *Therapeutae,* belonging to a sect described by Philo of Alexandria (*De Vita Contemplativa,* 21–90), were dedicated to contemplation and sought wisdom.

It does not seem that Mary ever knew about these Jewish religious groups which practiced the ideal of celibacy and virginity. But the fact that John the Baptist probably lived a celibate life and that in the community of his disciples it was held in high esteem would support the supposition that Mary's choice of virginity belonged to this new cultural and religious context.

However, the extraordinary case of the Virgin of Nazareth must not lead us into the error of tying her inner dispositions completely to the mentality of her surroundings, thereby eliminating the uniqueness of the mystery that came to pass in her. In particular, we must not forget that, from the very beginning of her life, Mary received a wondrous grace, recognized by the angel at the moment of the annunciation. "Full of grace" (Lk 1:28), Mary was enriched with a perfection of holiness that, according to the Church's interpretation, goes back to the very first moment of her existence. The unique privilege of the immaculate conception influenced the whole development of the young woman of Nazareth's spiritual life.

Thus, it should be maintained that Mary was guided to the ideal of virginity by an exceptional inspiration of that same Holy Spirit who, in the course of the Church's history, would spur many women to the way of virginal consecration. The singular presence of grace in Mary's life leads to the conclusion that the young girl was committed to virginity. Filled with the Lord's exceptional gifts from the beginning of her life, she was oriented to a total gift of self—body and soul—to God, in the offering of herself as a virgin.

In addition, her aspiration to the virginal life was in harmony with that "poverty" before God which the Old Testament holds in high esteem. Fully committing herself to this path, Mary also gave up motherhood, woman's personal treasure, so deeply appreciated in Israel. Thus she "stands out among the poor and humble of the Lord, who confidently hope for and receive salvation from him" (*LG* 55). However, presenting herself to God as poor and aiming only at spiritual fruitfulness, the fruit of divine love, at the moment of the annunciation Mary discovered that the Lord had transformed her poverty into riches: she would be the virgin Mother of the Son of the Most High. Later she would also discover that her motherhood is destined to extend to all men, whom the Son came to save (cf. *CCC* 501).

General audience of July 24, 1996

The Eternal Son of God
Is Also Born of Mary

In his saving plan, God wanted his only Son to be born of a virgin. This divine decision calls for a profound relationship between Mary's virginity and the Incarnation of the Word. "The eyes of faith can discover in the context of the whole of revelation the mysterious reasons why God in his saving plan wanted his Son to be born of a virgin. These reasons touch both on the person of Christ and his redemptive mission and on the welcome Mary gave that mission on behalf of all men" (*CCC* 502).

By excluding human fatherhood, the virginal conception affirms that Jesus' only Father is the heavenly Father and that the Son's being born in time reflects his eternal birth. The Father, who begot the Son in eternity, also begets him in time as a man.

The annunciation account emphasizes his state as "Son of God," the result of God's intervention in his conception. "The Holy Spirit will come upon you, and the power of the Most High will overshadow you; therefore, the child to be born will be called holy, the 'Son of God'" (Lk 1:35).

He who is born of Mary is already Son of God by virtue of his eternal birth. His virginal birth, brought about by the Most High, shows that he is Son of God even in his humanity. The revelation of his eternal birth in his virginal birth is also suggested by the passages in the Prologue of John's Gospel which relate the manifestation of the invisible God to the work of "the only Son, who is in the bosom of the Father" (1:18), by his coming in the flesh: "And the Word became flesh and dwelt among us; we have beheld his glory, glory as of the only Son from the Father, full of grace and truth" (Jn 1:14).

In recounting the birth of Jesus, Luke and Matthew also speak of the role of the Holy Spirit. The latter is not the father of the child. Jesus is the Son of the Eternal Father alone (cf. Lk 1:32–35), who through the Spirit is at work in the world and begets the Word in his human nature. Indeed, at the annunciation the angel calls the Spirit "the power of the Most High" (Lk 1:35), in harmony with the Old Testament, which presents him as the divine energy at work in human life, making it capable of marvelous deeds. Manifesting itself to the supreme degree in the mystery of the Incarnation, this power, which in the trinitarian life of God is Love, has the task of giving humanity the incarnate Word. The Holy Spirit, in particular, is the person who communicates divine riches to men and makes them sharers in God's life. He, who in the mystery of the Trinity is the unity of the Father and the Son, unites humanity with God by bringing about the virginal birth of Jesus.

The mystery of the Incarnation also highlights the incomparable greatness of Mary's virginal motherhood: the conception of Jesus is the fruit of her generous cooperation with the action of the Spirit of Love, the source of all fruitfulness. In the divine plan of salvation, the virginal conception is therefore an announcement of the new creation: by the work of the Holy Spirit, he who will be the new Adam is begotten in Mary. As the *Catechism of the Catholic Church* states: "Jesus is conceived by the Holy Spirit in the Virgin Mary's womb because he is the New Adam, who inaugurates the new creation" (n. 504).

The role of Mary's virginal motherhood shines forth in the mystery of this new creation. Calling Christ "the firstborn of the Virgin" (*Adv. Haer.,* 3, 16, 4), St. Irenaeus recalls that after Jesus many others are born of the Virgin, in the sense that they receive the new life of Christ. "Jesus is Mary's only son, but her spiritual motherhood extends to all men whom indeed he came to save: 'the Son whom she brought forth is he whom God placed as the firstborn among many brethren, that is, the faithful in whose generation and formation she cooperates with a mother's love'" (*CCC* 501, quoting *LG*).

The communication of the new life is the transmission of divine sonship. Here we can recall the perspective John opens up in the Prologue of his Gospel: he who was begotten by God gives all believers the power to become children of God (cf. Jn 1:12–13). The virginal birth allows the extension of the divine fatherhood: men are made the adoptive children of God in him who is Son of the Virgin and of the Father. Contemplating the mystery of the virgin birth thus enables us to realize that God chose a virgin Mother for his Son to offer his fatherly love more generously to humanity.

General audience of July 31, 1996

Mary's Choice
Inspires Consecrated Virginity

The intention to remain a virgin, apparent in Mary's words at the moment of the annunciation, has traditionally been considered the beginning and the inspiration of Christian virginity in the Church.

St. Augustine did not see in this resolution the fulfillment of a divine precept, but a vow freely taken. In the way it was possible to present Mary as an example to "holy virgins" throughout the Church's history. Mary "dedicated her virginity to God when she did not yet know whom she would conceive, so that the imitation of heavenly life in the earthly, mortal body would come about through a vow, not a precept, through a choice of love and not through the need to serve" (*De Sancta Virg.,* IV, *PL* 40:398).

The angel did not ask Mary to remain a virgin; it was Mary who freely revealed her intention of virginity. The choice of love that led her to consecrate herself totally to the Lord by a life of virginity is found in this commitment. In stressing the spontaneity of Mary's decision, we must not forget that God's initiative is at the root of every vocation. By choosing the life of virginity, the young girl of Nazareth was responding to an interior call, that is, to an inspiration of the Holy Spirit that enlightened her about the meaning and value of the virginal gift of herself. No one can accept this gift without feeling called or without receiving from the Holy Spirit the necessary light and strength.

Although St. Augustine used the word "vow" to show those he called "holy virgins" the first example of their state of life, the Gospel does not testify that Mary had expressly made a vow. This form of consecration and offering of one's life to God has been in use since the early centuries of the Church. From the Gospel we learn that Mary made a personal decision to remain a virgin, offering her heart to the Lord. She wanted to be his faithful bride, fulfilling her vocation as the "Daughter of Zion." By her decision, however, she became the archetype of all those in the Church who have chosen to serve the Lord with an undivided heart in virginity.

Neither the Gospels nor any other New Testament writings tell us when Mary decided to remain a virgin. However, it is clearly apparent from her question to the angel at the time of the annunciation that she had come to a very firm decision. Mary did not hesitate to express her desire to preserve her virginity even in view of the proposed motherhood, showing that her intention had matured over a long period.

Indeed, Mary's choice of virginity was not made in the unforeseeable prospect of becoming the Mother of God, but developed in her consciousness before the annunciation. We can suppose that this inclination was always present in her heart: the grace which prepared her for virginal motherhood certainly influenced the whole growth of her personality, while the Holy Spirit did not fail to inspire in her, from her earliest years, the desire for total union with God.

The marvels God still works today in the hearts and lives of so many young people were first realized in Mary's soul. Even in our world, so distracted by the attractions of a frequently superficial and consumerist culture, many adolescents accept the invitation that comes from Mary's example and consecrate their youth to the Lord and to the service of their brothers and sisters.

This decision is the choice of greater values, rather than the renunciation of human values. In this regard, in his Apostolic Exhortation *Marialis Cultus* my venerable Predecessor Paul VI emphasized how anyone who looks at the witness of the Gospel with an open mind "will appreciate that Mary's choice of the state of virginity...was not a rejection of any of the values of the married state but a courageous choice which she made in order to consecrate herself totally to the love of God" (n. 37).

In short, the choice of the virginal state is motivated by full adherence to Christ. This is particularly obvious in Mary. Although before the annunciation she was not conscious of it, the Holy Spirit inspired her virginal consecration in view of Christ. Mary remained a virgin to welcome the Messiah and Savior with her whole being. The virginity begun in Mary thus reveals its own Christocentric dimension, essential also for virginity lived in the Church, which finds its sublime model in the Mother of Christ. If her personal virginity, linked to the divine motherhood, remains an exceptional fact, it gives light and meaning to every gift of virginity.

How many young women in the Church's history, as they contemplated the nobility and beauty of the virginal heart of the Lord's Mother, have felt encouraged to respond generously to God's call by embracing the ideal of virginity! "Precisely such virginity," as I recalled in the Encyclical *Redemptoris Mater,* "after the example of the Virgin of Nazareth, is the source of a special spiritual fruitfulness: it is the source of motherhood in the Holy Spirit" (n. 43).

Mary's virginal life inspires in the entire Christian people esteem for the gift of virginity and the desire that it should increase in the Church as a sign of God's primacy over all reality and as a prophetic anticipation of the life to come. Together let us thank the Lord for those who still today generously consecrate their lives in virginity to the service of the kingdom of God.

At the same time, while in various regions evangelized long ago hedonism and consumerism seem to dissuade many young people from embracing the consecrated life, we must incessantly ask God through Mary's intercession for a new flowering of religious vocations. Thus the face of Christ's Mother, reflected in the many virgins who strive to follow the divine Master, will continue to be the sign of God's mercy and tenderness for humanity.

General audience of August 7, 1996

Mary and Joseph
Lived the Gift of Virginity

In presenting Mary as a "virgin," the Gospel of Luke adds that she was "betrothed to a man whose name was Joseph, of the house of David" (Lk 1:27). These two pieces of information at first sight seem contradictory. The Greek word used in this passage does not indicate the situation of a woman who has contracted marriage and therefore lives in the marital state, but that of betrothal. Unlike what occurs in modern cultures, however, the ancient Jewish custom of betrothal provided for a contract and normally had definitive value. It actually introduced the betrothed to the marital state, even if the marriage was brought to full completion only when the young man took the girl to his home.

At the time of the annunciation Mary thus had the status of one betrothed. We can wonder why she would accept betrothal, since she had the intention of remaining a virgin forever. Luke is aware of this difficulty, but merely notes the situation without offering any explanation. The fact that the evangelist, while stressing Mary's intention of virginity, also presents her as Joseph's spouse, is a sign of the historical reliability of the two pieces of information.

It may be presumed that at the time of their betrothal there was an understanding between Joseph and Mary about the plan to live as a virgin. Moreover, the Holy Spirit, who had inspired Mary to choose virginity in view of the mystery of the Incarnation and who wanted the latter to come about in a family setting suited to the child's growth, was quite able to instill in Joseph the ideal of virginity as well.

The angel of the Lord appeared in a dream and said to him: "Joseph, son of David, do not fear to take Mary your wife, for that which is conceived in her is of the Holy Spirit" (Mt 1:20). Thus, he received confirmation that he was called to live his marriage in a completely special way. Through virginal communion with the woman chosen to give birth to Jesus, God called him to cooperate in carrying out his plan of salvation.

The type of marriage to which the Holy Spirit led Mary and Joseph can only be understood in the context of the saving plan and of a lofty spirituality. The concrete realization of the mystery of the Incarnation called for a virgin birth which would highlight the divine sonship. At the same time, it called for a family that could provide for the normal development of the child's personality.

Precisely in view of their contribution to the mystery of the Incarnation of the Word, Joseph and Mary received the grace of living both the charism of virginity and the gift of marriage. Mary and Joseph's communion of virginal love, although a special case linked with the concrete realization of the mystery of the Incarnation, was nevertheless a true marriage (cf. Apostolic Exhortation *Redemptoris Custos,* 7).

The difficulty of accepting the sublime mystery of their spousal communion has led some, since the second century, to think of Joseph as advanced in age and to consider him Mary's guardian more than her husband. It is instead a case of supposing that he was not an elderly man at the time, but that his interior perfection, the fruit of grace, led him to live his spousal relationship with Mary with virginal affection.

Joseph's cooperation in the mystery of the Incarnation also includes exercising the role of Jesus' father. The angel acknowledged this function when he appeared in a dream and invited Joseph to name the child: "She will bear a son, and you shall call his name Jesus, for he will save his people from their sins" (Mt 1:21).

While excluding physical generation, Joseph's fatherhood was something real, not apparent. Distinguishing between father and the one who begets, an ancient monograph on Mary's virginity, the *De Margarita* (fourth century), states that "the commitments assumed by the Virgin and by Joseph as husband and wife made it possible for him to be called by this name [father], a father, however, who did not beget." Joseph thus carried out the role of Jesus' father, exercising an authority to which the redeemer was freely "obedient" (Lk 2:51), contributing to his upbringing and teaching him the carpenter's trade.

Christians have always acknowledged Joseph as the one who lived in intimate communion with Mary and Jesus, concluding that also in death he enjoyed their affectionate, consoling presence. From this constant Christian tradition, in many places a special devotion has grown to the holy family and, in it, to St. Joseph, guardian of the Redeemer. As everyone knows, Pope Leo XIII entrusted the entire Church to his protection.

General audience of August 21, 1996

The Church Presents
Mary As Ever-Virgin

The Church has always professed her belief in the perpetual virginity of Mary. The most ancient texts, when referring to the conception of Jesus, call Mary simply "virgin," inferring that they considered this quality a permanent fact with regard to her whole life. The early Christians expressed this conviction of faith in the Greek term *aeiparthenos*—"ever-virgin"—created to describe Mary's person in a unique and effective manner, and to express in a single word the Church's belief in her perpetual virginity. We find it used in the second symbol of faith composed by St. Epiphanius in 374, in relation to the Incarnation: the Son of God "was incarnate, that is, he was generated in a perfect way by Mary, the ever blessed Virgin through the Holy Spirit" (*Ancoratus,* 119, 5; *DS* 44).

The Second Council of Constantinople (553) took up the expression "ever-virgin" and affirmed: the Word of God, "incarnate of the holy and glorious Mother of God and ever-virgin Mary, was born of her" (*DS* 422). This doctrine is confirmed by two other ecumenical councils, the Fourth Lateran Council (1215; *DS* 801) and the Second Council of Lyons (1274; *DS* 852), and by the text of the definition of the dogma of the assumption (1950; *DS* 3903). In this text, Mary's perpetual virginity is adopted as one of the reasons why she was taken up in body and soul to heavenly glory.

In a brief formula, the Church traditionally presents Mary as "virgin before, during and after giving birth," affirming, by indicating these three moments, that she never ceased to be a virgin. Of the three, the affirmation of her virginity "before giving birth" is undoubtedly the most important, because it refers to Jesus' conception and directly touches the mystery of the Incarnation. From the beginning it has been constantly present in the Church's belief.

Her virginity "during and after giving birth," although implicit in the title "Virgin" already attributed to Mary from the Church's earliest days, became the object of deep doctrinal study since some began explicitly to cast doubts on it. Pope St. Hormisdas explained that "the Son of God became Son of man, born in time in the manner of a man, opening his mother's womb to birth [cf. Lk 2:23], and through God's power, not dissolving his mother's virginity" (*DS* 368). The Second Vatican Council confirmed this doctrine, and stated that the firstborn Son of Mary "did not diminish his Mother's virginal integrity but sanctified it" (*LG* 57). As regards her virginity after the birth, it must first of all be pointed out that there are no reasons for thinking that the will to remain a virgin, which Mary expressed at the moment of the annunciation (cf. Lk 1:34) was then changed. Moreover, the immediate meaning of the words "Woman, behold, your son!" "Behold, your mother" (Jn 19:26), which Jesus addressed from the cross to Mary and to his favorite disciple, imply that Mary had no other children.

Those who deny her virginity after the birth thought they had found a convincing argument in the term "firstborn," attributed to Jesus in the Gospel (Lk 2:7), almost as though this word implied that Mary had borne other children after Jesus. But the word "firstborn" literally means "a child not preceded by another" and, in itself, makes no reference to the existence of other children. Moreover, the evangelist stressed this characteristic of the child since certain obligations proper to Jewish law were linked to the birth of the firstborn son, independently of whether the mother might have given birth to other children. Thus, every only son was subject to these prescriptions because he was "begotten first" (cf. Lk 2:23).

According to some, Mary's virginity after the birth is denied by the Gospel texts which record the existence of four "brothers of Jesus": James, Joseph, Simon and Judas (Mt 13:55–56; Mk 6:3) and of several sisters. It should be recalled that no specific term exists in Hebrew and Aramaic to express the word "cousin," and that the terms "brother" and "sister" therefore included several degrees of relationship. The phrase "brothers of Jesus" indicates "the children" of a Mary who was a disciple of Christ (cf. Mt 27:56) and who is significantly described as "the other Mary" (Mt 28:1). "They are close relations of Jesus, according to an Old Testament expression" (*CCC* 500).

Mary Most Holy is thus the "ever-virgin." Her prerogative is the consequence of her divine motherhood which totally consecrated her to Christ's mission of redemption.

General audience of August 28, 1996

Mary Offers a Sublime Model of Service

Mary's words at the annunciation, "I am the handmaid of the Lord; let it be to me according to your word" (Lk 1:38), indicate an attitude characteristic of Jewish piety. At the beginning of the Old Covenant, Moses, in response to the Lord's call, proclaimed himself the Lord's servant (cf. Ex 4:10; 14:31). With the coming of the New Covenant, Mary also responded to God with an act of free submission and conscious abandonment to his will, showing her complete availability to be the "handmaid of the Lord."

In the Old Testament, the qualification "servant" of God links all those who are called to exercise a mission for the sake of the Chosen People: Abraham (Gn 26:24), Isaac (Gn 24:14), Jacob (Ex 32:13; Ez 37:25), Joshua (Jos 24:29), David (2 Sm 7, 8, etc.). Prophets and priests, who have been entrusted with the task of forming the people in the faithful service of the Lord, are also servants. In the docility of the "suffering Servant," the Book of Isaiah exalts a model of fidelity to God in the hope of redemption for the sins of the many (cf. Is 42:53). Some women also offer examples of fidelity, such as Queen Esther who, before interceding for the salvation of the Jews, addressed a prayer to God, calling herself many times "your servant" (Est 4:17).

By proclaiming herself "handmaid of the Lord," Mary, "full of grace," intended to commit herself to fulfill personally and in a perfect manner the service God expects of all his people. The words: "Behold, I am the handmaid of the Lord," foretell the one who will say of himself: "The Son of Man also came not to be served but to serve, and to give his life as a ransom for many" (Mk 10:45; cf. Mt 20:28). Thus, the Holy Spirit brings about a harmony of intimate dispositions between the Mother and the Son which will allow Mary to assume fully her maternal role to Jesus, as she accompanies him in his mission as servant. In Jesus' life the will to serve is constant and surprising. As Son of God, he could rightly have demanded to be served. Attributing to himself the title "Son of Man," whom, according to the Book of Daniel, "all peoples, nations and languages should serve" (Dn 7:14), he could have claimed mastery over others. Instead, combating the mentality of the time which was expressed in the disciples' ambition for the first places (cf. Mk 9:34) and in Peter's protest during the washing of the feet (cf. Jn 13:6), Jesus did not want to be served. He desired to serve to the point of totally giving his life in the work of redemption.

Furthermore, Mary spontaneously declared herself "the handmaid of the Lord," although aware of the lofty dignity conferred upon her at the angel's announcement. In this commitment of service she also included the intention to serve her neighbor, as the link between the episodes of the annunciation and the visitation show. Informed by the angel of Elizabeth's pregnancy, Mary set out "with haste" (Lk 1:39) for Judah, with total availability to help her relative prepare for the birth. She thus offers Christians of all times a sublime model of service.

The words: "Let it be to me according to your word" (Lk 1:38) show in Mary, who declared herself handmaid of the Lord, a total obedience to God's will. Luke uses the optative *genoito,* "let it be done," which expresses not only acceptance but staunch assumption of the divine plan, making it her own with the involvement of all her personal resources.

By conforming to the divine will, Mary anticipated and made her own the attitude of Christ. According to the Letter to the Hebrews, coming into the world, he said: "Sacrifice and offerings you did not desire, but a body you prepared for me.... Then I said...'Behold, I come to do your will, O God'" (Heb 10:5–7; Ps 39:7–9).

Mary's docility likewise announced and prefigured that which Jesus expressed in the course of his public life until Calvary. Christ would say: "My food is to do the will of him who sent me, and to accomplish his work" (Jn 4:34). On these same lines, Mary made the Father's will the inspiring principle of her whole life, seeking in it the necessary strength to fulfill the mission entrusted to her.

If at the moment of the annunciation Mary did not yet know of the sacrifice which would mark Christ's mission, Simeon's prophecy enabled her to glimpse her Son's tragic destiny (cf. Lk 3:34–35). The Virgin would be associated with him in intimate sharing. With her total obedience to God's will, Mary was ready to live all that divine love would plan for her life, even to the "sword" that would pierce her soul.

General audience of September 4, 1996

Mary, the New Eve, Freely Obeyed God

Commenting on the episode of the annunciation, the Second Vatican Council gave special emphasis to the value of Mary's assent to the divine messenger's words. Unlike what occurs in similar biblical accounts, it was expressly awaited by the angel: "The Father of mercies willed that the Incarnation should be preceded by the acceptance of her who was predestined to be the mother of his Son, so that just as a woman contributed to death, so also a woman should contribute to life" (*LG* 56).

Lumen Gentium recalls the contrast between Eve's behavior and Mary's, described by St. Irenaeus: "Just as the former—that is, Eve—was seduced by the words of an angel so that she turned away from God by disobeying his word, so the latter—Mary—received the good news from an angel's announcement in such a way as to give birth to God by obeying his word. And as the former was seduced so that she disobeyed God, the latter let herself be convinced to obey God, and so the Virgin Mary became the advocate of the virgin Eve. As the human race was subjected to death by a virgin, it was liberated by a virgin; a virgin's disobedience was thus counterbalanced by a virgin's obedience..." (*Adv. Haer.,* V, 19, 1).

In stating her total "yes" to the divine plan, Mary was completely free before God. At the same time, she felt personally responsible for humanity, whose future was linked with her reply.

God put the destiny of all mankind in a young woman's hands. Mary's "yes" was the premise for fulfilling the plan which God in his love had prepared for the world's salvation. The *Catechism of the Catholic Church* briefly and effectively summarizes the decisive value for all humanity of Mary's free consent to the divine plan of salvation. "The Virgin Mary 'cooperated through free faith and obedience in human salvation' (*LG* 56). She uttered her yes 'in the name of all human nature' (St. Thomas Aquinas, *STh* III, 30, 1). By her obedience she became the New Eve, mother of the living" (n. 511).

By her conduct, Mary reminds each of us of our serious responsibility to accept God's plan for our lives. In total obedience to the saving will of God expressed in the angel's words, she became a model for those whom the Lord proclaims blessed, because they "hear the word of God and keep it" (Lk 11:28). In answering the woman in the crowd who proclaimed his mother blessed, Jesus disclosed the true reason for Mary's blessedness: her adherence to God's will, which led her to accept the divine motherhood. In the Encyclical *Redemptoris Mater* I pointed out that the new spiritual motherhood of which Jesus spoke is primarily concerned with her. Indeed, "Is not Mary the first of 'those who hear the word of God and do it'? And therefore does not the blessing uttered by Jesus in response to the woman in the crowd refer primarily to her?" (*RM* 20). In a certain sense, therefore, Mary is proclaimed the first disciple of her Son (cf. *RM* 20), and by her example invites all believers to respond generously to the Lord's grace.

The Second Vatican Council explained Mary's total dedication to the person and work of Christ: "She devoted herself totally as a handmaid of the Lord to the person and work of her Son, under him and with him, by the grace of almighty God, serving the mystery of redemption" (*LG* 56). For Mary, dedication to the person and work of Jesus means intimate union with her Son, motherly involvement in nurturing his human growth and cooperation with his work of salvation.

Mary carries out this last aspect of her dedication to Jesus "under him," that is, in a condition of subordination, which is the fruit of grace. However, this is true cooperation, because it is realized "with him," and beginning with the annunciation, it involves active participation in the work of redemption. "Rightly, therefore," the Second Vatican Council observed, "the holy Fathers see her as used by God not merely in a passive way, but as freely cooperating in the work of human salvation through faith and obedience. For, as St. Irenaeus says, she 'being obedient, became the cause of salvation for herself and for the whole human race' (*Adv. Haer.*, III, 22, 4)" (*LG* 56).

Associated with Christ's victory over the sin of our first parents, Mary appears as the true "mother of the living" (*LG* 56). Her motherhood, freely accepted in obedience to the divine plan, becomes a source of life for all humanity.

General audience of September 18, 1996

The Visitation
Is a Prelude to Jesus' Mission

In the visitation episode, St. Luke shows how the grace of the Incarnation, after filling Mary, brings salvation and joy to Elizabeth's house. Carried in his Mother's womb, the Savior of men pours out the Holy Spirit, revealing himself from the start of his coming into the world. In describing Mary's departure for Judea, the evangelist uses the verb *anístemi,* which means "to arise," "to start moving." Considering that this verb is used in the Gospels to indicate Jesus' resurrection (Mk 8:31; 9:9, 31; Lk 24:7, 46) or physical actions that imply a spiritual effort (Lk 5:27–28; 15:18, 20), we can suppose that Luke wished to stress with this expression the vigorous zeal which led Mary, under the inspiration of the Holy Spirit, to give the world its Savior.

The Gospel text also reports that Mary made the journey "with haste" (Lk 1:39). In the Lucan context, even the note "into the hill country" (Lk 1:39) appears to be much more than a simple topographical indication, since it calls to mind the messenger of good news described in the Book of Isaiah: "How beautiful upon the mountains are the feet of him who brings good tidings, who announces peace, who bears good news, who announces salvation, who says to Zion: 'Your God reigns'" (Is 52:7).

Like St. Paul, who recognized the fulfillment of this prophetic text in the preaching of the Gospel (Rom 10:15), St. Luke also seems to invite us to see Mary as the first "evangelist," who spreads the "good news," initiating the missionary journeys of her divine Son. Lastly, the direction of the Blessed Virgin's journey is particularly significant: it will be from Galilee to Judea, like Jesus' missionary journey (cf. 9:51). Mary's visit to Elizabeth is a prelude to Jesus' mission, and in cooperating from the beginning of her motherhood in the Son's redeeming work, she became the model for those in the Church who set out to bring Christ's light and joy to the people of every time and place.

The meeting with Elizabeth has the character of a joyous saving event that goes beyond the spontaneous feelings of family sentiment. Where the embarrassment of disbelief seems to be expressed in Zechariah's muteness, Mary burst out with the joy of her quick and ready faith: "She entered the house of Zechariah and greeted Elizabeth" (Lk 1:40).

St. Luke relates that "when Elizabeth heard the greeting of Mary, the babe leaped in her womb" (Lk 1:41). Mary's greeting caused Elizabeth's son to leap for joy. Jesus' entrance into Elizabeth's house, at Mary's doing, brought the unborn prophet that gladness which the Old Testament foretells as a sign of the Messiah's presence. At Mary's greeting, messianic joy came over Elizabeth too, and "filled with the Holy Spirit...she exclaimed with a loud cry, 'Blessed are you among women, and blessed is the fruit of your womb!'" (Lk 1:41–42). By a higher light, she understood Mary's greatness: more than Jael and Judith, who prefigured her in the Old Testament, she is blessed among women because of the fruit of her womb, Jesus the Messiah.

Elizabeth's exclamation, made "with a loud cry," shows a true religious enthusiasm. This continues to be echoed on the lips of believers in the prayer "Hail Mary," as the Church's song of praise for the great works the Most High accomplished in the Mother of his Son. In proclaiming her "blessed among women," Elizabeth pointed to Mary's faith as the reason for her blessedness: "And blessed is she who believed that there would be a fulfillment of what was spoken to her from the Lord" (Lk 1:45). Mary's greatness and joy arise from the fact that she is the one who believes.

In view of Mary's excellence, Elizabeth also understood what an honor this visit was for her: "And why is this granted me, that the mother of my Lord should come to me?" (Lk 1:43). With the expression "my Lord," Elizabeth recognized the royal messianic dignity of Mary's Son. In the Old Testament this expression was used to address the king (cf. 1 Kgs 1:13, 20, 21, etc.) and to speak of the Messiah King (Ps 110:1). The angel had said of Jesus: "The Lord God will give to him the throne of his father David" (Lk 1:32). "Filled with the Holy Spirit," Elizabeth had the same insight. Later, the paschal glorification of Christ would reveal the sense in which this title is to be understood, that is, a transcendent sense (cf. Jn 20:28; Acts 2:34–36).

With her admiring exclamation, Elizabeth invites us to appreciate all that the Virgin's presence brings as a gift to the life of every believer. In the visitation, the Virgin brought Christ to the Baptist's mother, the Christ who pours out the Holy Spirit. This role of mediatrix is brought out by Elizabeth's very words: "For behold, when the voice of your greeting came to my ears, the babe in my womb leaped for joy" (Lk 1:44). By the gift of the Holy Spirit, Mary's presence serves as a prelude to Pentecost, confirming a cooperation which, having begun with the Incarnation, is destined to be expressed in the whole work of divine salvation.

General audience of October 2, 1996

Mary Sings the Praises of God's Mercy

Inspired by the Old Testament tradition with the song of the Magnificat, Mary celebrated the marvels God worked in her. This song is the Virgin's response to the mystery of the annunciation; the angel had invited her to rejoice and Mary expressed the exultation of her spirit in God her Savior. Her joy flowed from the personal experience of God's looking with kindness upon her, a poor creature with no historical influence.

The word "Magnificat," the Latin version of a Greek word with the same meaning, celebrates the greatness of God. He reveals his omnipotence through the angel's message, surpassing the expectations and hopes of the people of the Covenant, and even the noblest aspirations of the human soul.

In the presence of the powerful and merciful Lord, Mary expressed her own sense of lowliness: "My soul magnifies the Lord and my spirit rejoices in God my Savior, for he has regarded the low estate of his handmaiden" (Lk 1:47–48). The Greek word *tapeínosis* is probably borrowed from the song of Hannah, Samuel's mother. It calls attention to the "humiliation" and "misery" of a barren woman (cf. 1 Sm 1:11), who confides her pain to the Lord. With a similar expression, Mary made known her situation of poverty and her awareness of being little before God, who by a free decision looked upon her, a humble girl from Nazareth, and called her to become the Mother of the Messiah.

The words "henceforth all generations will call me blessed" (Lk 1:48) arise from the fact that Elizabeth was the first to proclaim Mary "blessed" (Lk 1:45). Not without daring, the song predicts that this same proclamation will be extended and increased with relentless momentum. At the same time it testifies to the special veneration for the Mother of Jesus which has been present in the Christian community from the first century. The Magnificat is the first fruit of the various forms of devotion, passed on from one generation to the next, in which the Church has expressed her love for the Virgin of Nazareth.

"For he who is mighty has done great things for me and holy is his name. And his mercy is on those who fear him from generation to generation" (Lk 1:49–50). What are the "great things" that the Almighty accomplished in Mary? The expression recurs in the Old Testament to indicate the deliverance of the people of Israel from Egypt or Babylon. In the Magnificat it refers to the mysterious event of Jesus' virginal conception, which occurred in Nazareth after the angel's announcement.

The Magnificat is a truly theological song because it reveals the experience Mary had of God's looking upon her. In it, God is not only the almighty to whom nothing is impossible, as Gabriel had declared (cf. Lk 1:37), but also the merciful, capable of tenderness and fidelity toward every human being.

"He has shown strength with his arm; he has scattered the proud in the imagination of their hearts; he has put down the mighty from their thrones, and exalted those of low degree; he has filled the hungry with good things and the rich he has sent empty away" (Lk 1:51–53). With her wise reading of history, Mary leads us to discover the criteria of God's mysterious action. Overturning the judgments of the world, he comes to the aid of the poor and lowly, to the detriment of the rich and powerful. In a surprising way he fills with good things the humble who entrust their lives to him (cf. *RM* 37). While these words of the song show us Mary as a concrete and sublime model, they give us to understand that humility of heart especially attracts God's kindness.

Lastly, the song exalts the fulfillment of God's promises and his fidelity to the Chosen People: "He has helped his servant Israel, in remembrance of his mercy, as he spoke to our fathers, to Abraham and to his posterity for ever" (Lk 1:54–55). Filled with divine gifts, Mary did not limit her vision to her own personal case, but realized how these gifts show forth God's mercy toward all his people. In her, God fulfilled his promises with a superabundance of fidelity and generosity.

Inspired by the Old Testament and by the spirituality of the Daughter of Zion, the Magnificat surpasses the prophetic texts on which it is based, revealing in her who is "full of grace" the beginning of a divine intervention which far exceeds Israel's messianic hopes: the holy mystery of the Incarnation of the Word.

General audience of November 6, 1996

The Nativity Shows
Mary's Closeness to Jesus

In the story of Jesus' birth, the evangelist Luke recounts several facts that help us better understand the meaning of the event. He first mentions the census ordered by Caesar Augustus, which obliges Joseph, "of the house and lineage of David," and Mary his wife to go "to the city of David, which is called Bethlehem" (Lk 2:4). In informing us about the circumstances in which the journey and birth take place, the evangelist presents us with a situation of hardship and poverty, which lets us glimpse some basic characteristics of the messianic kingdom. It is a kingdom without earthly honors or powers, which belongs to him who, in his public life, will say of himself: "The Son of man has nowhere to lay his head" (Lk 9:58).

Luke's account contains a few seemingly unimportant notes, which are meant to arouse in the reader a better understanding of the mystery of the nativity and the sentiments of Mary, who gave birth to the Son of God. The description of the birth, recounted in simple fashion, presents Mary as intensely participating in what was taking place in her: "She gave birth to her firstborn son and wrapped him in swaddling clothes, and laid him in a manger..." (Lk 2:7). The Virgin's action was the result of her complete willingness to cooperate in God's plan, already expressed at the annunciation in her "let it be to me according to your word" (Lk 1:38). Mary experienced child-birth in a condition of extreme poverty. She could not give the Son of God even what mothers usually offer a newborn baby. Instead, she had to lay him "in a manger," an improvised cradle which contrasts with the dignity of the "Son of the Most High."

The Gospel notes that "there was no place for them in the inn" (Lk 2:7). This statement, recalling the text in John's Prologue: "His own people received him not" (Jn 1:11), foretells as it were the many refusals Jesus will meet with during his earthly life. The phrase "for them" joins the Son and the Mother in this rejection, and shows how Mary is already associated with her Son's destiny of suffering and shares in his redeeming mission. Rejected by "his own," Jesus was welcomed by the shepherds, unrefined men but chosen by God as the first to receive the good news of the Savior's birth. The message the angel gave them was an invitation to rejoice: "Behold, I bring you good news of a great joy which will come to all the people" (Lk 2:10), along with a request to overcome all fear: "Be not afraid."

Indeed, as it was for Mary at the time of the annunciation, so too for them the news of Jesus' birth represented the great sign of God's goodwill toward men. In the divine Redeemer, contemplated in the poverty of a Bethlehem cave, we can see an invitation to approach with confidence the one who is the hope of humanity. The angels' song: "Glory to God in the highest, and on earth peace among men with whom he is pleased!" which can also be translated as "men of goodwill" (Lk 2:14), revealed to the shepherds what Mary had expressed in her *Magnificat.* Jesus' birth is the sign of God's merciful love, which is especially shown toward the poor and humble.

The shepherds responded enthusiastically and promptly to the angel's invitation: "Let us go over to Bethlehem and see this thing that has happened, which the Lord has made known to us" (Lk 2:15). They did not search in vain: "And they...found

Mary and Joseph, and the babe" (Lk 2:16). To them, as the Council recalls, "the Mother of God joyfully showed her first-born Son" (*LG* 57). It was the defining moment of their lives.

The shepherds' spontaneous desire to make known what "had been told them concerning this child" (Lk 2:17), after the wondrous experience of meeting the Mother and her Son, suggests to evangelizers in every age the importance, and even more, the necessity of a deep spiritual relationship with Mary. This is in order to know Jesus better and to become the joyful proclaimers of his Gospel of salvation. With regard to these extraordinary events, Luke tells us that Mary "kept all these things, pondering them in her heart" (Lk 2:19). While the shepherds passed from fear to wonder and praise, the Virgin, because of her faith, kept alive the memory of the events involving her Son, and deepened her understanding of them by reflecting on them in her heart, that is, in the inmost core of her person. In this way she suggests that another mother, the Church, should foster the gift and task of contemplation and theological reflection, in order better to accept the mystery of salvation, to understand it more thoroughly and to proclaim it with renewed effort to the people of every age.

General audience of November 20, 1996

The Church Proclaims
Mary "Mother of God"

Contemplation of the mystery of the Savior's birth has led Christian people not only to invoke the Blessed Virgin as the Mother of Jesus, but also to recognize her as Mother of God. This truth was already confirmed and perceived as belonging to the Church's heritage of faith from the early centuries of the Christian era, until it was solemnly proclaimed at the Council of Ephesus in 431.

In the first Christian community, as the disciples became more aware that Jesus is the Son of God, it became ever clearer that Mary is the *Theotókos,* the Mother of God. This title does not appear explicitly in the Gospel texts, but in them the "Mother of Jesus" is mentioned and it is affirmed that Jesus is God (Jn 20:28; cf. 5:18; 10:30, 33). Mary is in any case presented as the Mother of Emmanuel, which means "God with us" (cf. Mt 1:22–23). Already in the third century, as can be deduced from an ancient written witness, the Christians of Egypt addressed this prayer to Mary: "We fly to thy patronage, O holy Mother of God; despise not our petitions in our necessities, but deliver us from all evil, O glorious and blessed Virgin" (from the *Liturgy of the Hours*). The expression *Theotókos* appears explicitly for the first time in this ancient witness.

In pagan mythology, it often happened that a certain goddess would be presented as the mother of some god. For example, the supreme god, Zeus, had the goddess Rhea as his mother. This context perhaps helped Christians to use the title *Theotókos*—Mother of God—for the Mother of Jesus. Nevertheless, it should be noted that this title did not exist but was created by Christians to express a belief which had nothing to do with pagan mythology, belief in the virginal conception in Mary's womb of the one who had always been the eternal Word of God.

By the fourth century, the term *Theotókos* was frequently used in the East and West. Devotion and theology refer more and more to this term, which had by now become part of the Church's patrimony of faith. One can therefore understand the great protest movement that arose in the fifth century when Nestorius cast doubt on the correctness of the title "Mother of God." Being inclined to hold that Mary was only the mother of the man Jesus, Nestorius maintained that "Mother of Christ" was the only doctrinally correct expression. He was led to make this error by his difficulty in admitting the unity of Christ's person and by his erroneous interpretation of the distinction between the two natures—divine and human—present in Christ. In 431 the Council of Ephesus condemned his theses, and in affirming the subsistence of the divine and human natures in the one person of the Son, proclaimed Mary the Mother of God.

The difficulties and objections Nestorius raised offer us the opportunity to make several useful reflections for correctly understanding and interpreting this title. The expression *Theotókos,* which literally means, "she who has begotten God," can at first sight seem surprising. It raises the question as to how it is possible for a human creature to give birth to God. The answer of the Church's faith is clear: Mary's divine motherhood refers only to the human begetting of the Son of God but not to his divine birth. The Son of God was eternally begotten of God the Father, and is consubstantial with him. Mary, of course, has no part in this eternal birth. However, the Son of God assumed our human nature 2000 years ago and was conceived by and born of Mary.

In proclaiming Mary "Mother of God," the Church thus intends to affirm that Mary is the "Mother of the incarnate Word, who is God." Her motherhood does not, therefore, extend to all the Trinity, but only to the second person, the Son, who, in becoming incarnate took his human nature from her. Motherhood is a relationship of person to person: a mother is not only mother of the body or of the physical creature born of her womb, but of the person she begets. Thus, having given birth according to his human nature to the person of Jesus, who is a divine person, Mary is the Mother of God.

In proclaiming Mary "Mother of God," the Church in a single phrase professes her belief regarding the Son and the Mother. This union was already seen at the Council of Ephesus. In defining Mary's divine motherhood, the Fathers intended to emphasize their belief in the divinity of Christ. Despite ancient and recent objections about the appropriateness of recognizing Mary by this title, Christians of all times, by correctly interpreting the meaning of this motherhood, have made it a privileged expression of their faith in the divinity of Christ and their love for the Blessed Virgin.

On the one hand, the Church recognizes the *Theotókos* as guaranteeing the reality of the Incarnation because—as St. Augustine says—"if the Mother were fictitious, the flesh would also be fictitious...and the scars of the resurrection" (*Tract. in Ev. Ioannis,* 8, 6–7). On the other hand, she also contemplates with wonder and celebrates with veneration the immense greatness conferred on Mary by the one who wanted to be her Son. The expression "Mother of God" is used as referring to the Word of God, who in the Incarnation assumed the lowliness of the human condition in order to raise man to divine sonship. But in the light of the sublime dignity conferred on the Virgin of Nazareth, this title also proclaims the nobility of woman and her loftiest vocation. God treated Mary as a free and responsible person and did not bring about the Incarnation of his Son until after he had obtained her consent.

Following the example of the ancient Christians of Egypt, let the faithful entrust themselves to Mary who, being the Mother of God, can obtain from her divine Son the grace of deliverance from evil and of eternal salvation.

General audience of November 27, 1996

The Blessed Virgin
Is a Model of Perfect Love

Although occurring by the work of the Holy Spirit and a virgin mother, the birth of Jesus, like that of all human beings, went through the phases of conception, gestation and delivery. In addition, Mary's motherhood was not limited to the biological process of giving birth. As it happens with every other mother, she also made an essential contribution to her son's growth and development. A mother is not only a woman who gives birth to a child, but one who brings him up and teaches him; indeed, we might well say that, according to God's plan, the educational task is the natural extension of procreation. Mary is the *Theotókos* not only because she conceived and gave birth to the Son of God, but also because she accompanied him in his human growth.

We might think that, since Jesus possessed in himself the fullness of divinity, he had no need of teachers. But the mystery of the Incarnation reveals to us that the Son of God came into the world in a human condition similar to us in all things except sin (cf. Heb 4:15). As is the case with every human being, Jesus' growth from infancy to adulthood (cf. Lk 2:40) also needed his parent's educational activity. The Gospel of Luke, particularly attentive to the childhood period, says that at Nazareth Jesus was obedient to Joseph and Mary (cf. Lk 2:51).

This dependence shows us that Jesus was receptive, open to the teaching of his mother and Joseph, who also carried out their task by virtue of the docility Jesus constantly showed.

The special gifts which God had showered on Mary made her particularly suited to her task as mother and teacher. In the concrete circumstances of everyday life, Jesus could find in her a model to follow and imitate and an example of perfect love for God and for his brothers and sisters. Along with Mary's motherly presence, Jesus could count on the paternal figure of Joseph, a just man (cf. Mt 1:19), who provided the necessary balance in the educational activity. Carrying out his role as father, Joseph cooperated with his wife in making the home in Nazareth an environment favorable to the growth and personal maturity of the Savior of humanity. By later introducing him to the hard work of the carpenter, Joseph enabled Jesus to be involved in the world of work and social life.

The few elements that the Gospel offers do not allow us to know and fully appreciate the ways in which Mary taught her divine Son. Certainly she, together with Joseph, introduced Jesus to the rites and prescriptions of Moses, to prayer to the God of the covenant by using the Psalms, to the history of the people of Israel centered on the Exodus from Egypt. From her and Joseph, Jesus learned to attend the synagogue and to make the annual pilgrimage to Jerusalem for the Passover. Looking at the results, we can certainly conclude that Mary's teaching was deep and effective, and found very fertile soil in Jesus' human psychology.

Mary's educational task with regard to such a unique son presents several special features in comparison with the role of other mothers. She only provided favorable conditions for the development of the potential and essential values for growth, already present in the Son. For example, the absence of any form of sin in Jesus demanded a constantly positive orientation from Mary, which excluded any form of corrective intervention. Furthermore, although his mother introduced Jesus to the culture and traditions of the people of Israel, from the time of his finding in the Temple he would reveal his full awareness of being the Son of God, sent to spread the truth in the world and exclusively follow the Father's will. From being her Son's "teacher," Mary thus became the humble disciple of the divine Master to whom she had given birth.

The importance of the virgin Mother's task remained; from his infancy to adulthood, she helped her Son Jesus to grow "in wisdom and in stature, and in favor with God and man" (Lk 2:52) and to prepare for his mission. Mary and Joseph can therefore be seen as models for all educators. They sustain them in the great difficulties that the family encounters today, and show them the way to their children's precise and effective formation. Their educational experience is a sure reference point for Christian parents who are called, in ever more complex and difficult conditions, to devote themselves to the service of the integral development of their children's personality, so that they will live lives worthy of man and corresponding to God's plan.

General audience of December 4, 1996

Simeon Was Open to the Lord's Action

In the episode of the presentation of Jesus in the Temple, St. Luke emphasizes Jesus' messianic destiny. According to the Lucan text, the immediate purpose of the holy family's journey from Bethlehem to Jerusalem was to fulfill the law: "And when the time came for their purification according to the law of Moses, they brought him up to Jerusalem to present him to the Lord (as it is written in the law of the Lord, 'Every male that opens the womb shall be called holy to the Lord'), and to offer a sacrifice according to what is said in the law of the Lord, 'a pair of turtledoves, or two young pigeons'" (Lk 2:22–24).

With this act, Mary and Joseph showed their intention of faithfully obeying God's will, rejecting every kind of privilege. Their coming to the Temple in Jerusalem had the significance of a consecration to God in the place where he is present. Obliged by her poverty to offer turtledoves or pigeons, Mary gave the true Lamb who would redeem humanity, thus anticipating what was prefigured in the ritual offerings of the old law.

While the law required the purification of the mother alone after birth, Luke speaks of the "time for *their* purification" (2:22), intending perhaps to indicate together the prescriptions involving both the mother and the firstborn Son.

The term "purification" can surprise us, because it is referred to a mother who had been granted, by a singular grace, to be immaculate from the first moment of her existence, and to a child who was totally holy. However, it must be remembered that it was not a question of purifying the conscience from some stain of sin. It only concerned reacquiring ritual purity which, according to the ideas of the time, may be harmed by the simple fact of birth without there being any form of guilt. The evangelist uses the occasion to stress the special link existing between Jesus, as "firstborn" (Lk 2:7, 23) and God's holiness, as well as to indicate the spirit of humble offering which motivated Mary and Joseph (cf. Lk 2:24). The "two turtledoves or two young pigeons" (Lv 12:8) was the offering of the poor.

In the Temple, Joseph and Mary met Simeon, "righteous and devout, looking for the consolation of Israel" (Lk 2:25). The Lucan narrative says nothing of his past or of the service he carried out in the Temple. It tells of a deeply religious man who nurtured great desires in his heart and awaited the Messiah, the consolation of Israel. "The Holy Spirit was upon him" and "it had been revealed to him...that he should not see death before he had seen the Lord's Christ" (Lk 2:25–26). Simeon invites us to look at the merciful action of God who pours out the Spirit on his faithful to bring to fulfillment his mysterious project of love.

Simeon, a man open to God's action, "inspired by the Spirit" (Lk 2:27), went to the Temple where he met Jesus, Joseph and Mary. Taking the child in his arms, he blessed God and said, "Lord, now let your servant depart in peace, according to your word" (Lk 2:29). Simeon used an Old Testament phrase to express the joy he experienced on meeting the Messiah and felt that the purpose of his life had been fulfilled. He could therefore ask the Most High to let him depart in peace to the next world.

In the episode of the presentation we can glimpse the meeting of Israel's hope with the Messiah. We can also see in it a prophetic sign of man's encounter with Christ. The Holy Spirit makes it possible by awakening in the human heart the desire for this salvific meeting and by bringing it about. Nor can we neglect the role of Mary who gave the child to the holy old man Simeon. By divine will, the Mother gives Jesus to mankind.

In revealing the Savior's future, Simeon referred to the prophecy of the "Servant" sent to the Chosen People and to the nations. To him the Lord says, "I have taken you by the hand and kept you; I have given you as a covenant to the people, a light to the nations" (Is 42:6). Again: "It is too light a thing that you should be my servant to raise up the tribes of Jacob and to restore the preserved of Israel; I will give you as a light to the nations, that my salvation may reach to the end of the earth" (Is 49:6).

In his canticle, Simeon reversed the perspective and stressed the universality of Jesus' mission: "For my eyes have seen your salvation which you have prepared in the presence of all peoples, a light for revelation to the Gentiles, and for the glory of your people Israel" (Lk 2:30–32).

How can we fail to marvel at these words? "And his father and mother marveled at what was said about him" (Lk 2:33). But this experience enabled Joseph and Mary to understand more clearly the importance of their act of offering. In the Temple of Jerusalem they presented the one who, being the glory of his people, is also the salvation of all mankind.

General audience of December 11, 1996

Mary Has a Role
in Jesus' Saving Mission

After recognizing in Jesus "a light for revelation to the Gentiles" (Lk 2:32), Simeon announced to Mary the great trial to which the Messiah was called and revealed her participation in that sorrowful destiny. Simeon's reference to the redeeming sacrifice, absent at the annunciation, has shown in his prophecy almost a "second annunciation" (*RM* 16), which will lead the Virgin to a deeper understanding of her Son's mystery.

Up to that moment Simeon had addressed all those present, blessing Joseph and Mary in particular. Then he prophesied to the Virgin alone that she would share in her Son's destiny. Inspired by the Holy Spirit, he announced to her: "Behold, this child is set for the fall and rising of many in Israel, and for a sign that is spoken against (and a sword will pierce through your own soul also), that thoughts out of many hearts may be revealed" (Lk 2:34–35).

These words foretell a future of suffering for the Messiah. He is "the sign of contradiction," destined to meet harsh opposition on the part of his contemporaries. But alongside Christ's suffering, Simeon set the vision of Mary's heart pierced by the sword, thus uniting the Mother with the sorrowful destiny of her Son.

In this way, while the venerable old man foresaw the grow-ing hostility the Messiah would face, he stressed its reper-cussion on the Mother's heart. This maternal suffering would culminate in the passion, when she would unite with her Son in his redemptive sacrifice.

Following an allusion to the first songs of the Servant of the Lord (cf. Is 42:6; 49:6) cited in Luke 2:32, Simeon's words remind us of the prophecy of the Suffering Servant (Is 52:13; 53:12). "Wounded for our transgressions" (Is 53:5), he "makes himself an offering for sin" (Is 53:10) through a personal and spiritual sacrifice which far exceeds the ancient ritual sacrifices. Here we can note how Simeon's prophecy allows us to glimpse in Mary's future suffering a unique likeness to the sorrowful future of the "Servant."

Mary and Joseph were astounded when Simeon proclaimed Jesus as a "light for revelation to the Gentiles" (Lk 2:32). With reference to the prophecy of the sword that would pierce her heart, Mary said nothing. Together with Joseph, she accepted in silence those mysterious words which predicted a deeply sor-rowful trial and situated the presentation of Jesus in the Temple in its most authentic meaning.

According to the divine plan, the sacrifice offered then "according to what is said in the law of the Lord, 'a pair of turtledoves, or two young pigeons'" (Lk 2:24), prefigured the sacrifice of Jesus, "for I am gentle and lowly of heart" (Mt 11:29). In it the true "presentation" would be made (cf. Lk 2:22), which would see the Mother associated with her Son in the work of redemption.

Simeon's prophecy was followed by the meeting with the prophetess Anna: "She gave thanks to God, and spoke of him to all who were looking for the redemption of Jerusalem" (Lk 2:38). The faith and prophetic wisdom of the old woman, who nurtured the expectation of the Messiah by "worshipping with fasting and prayer night and day" (Lk 2:37), offered the holy family a further incentive to put their hope in the God of Israel. At this particular moment, Anna's behavior would have appeared to Mary and Joseph as a sign from the Lord, a message of enlightened faith and persevering service. Beginning with Simeon's prophecy, Mary intensely and mysteriously united her life with Christ's sorrowful mission. She was to become her Son's faithful co-worker for the salvation of the human race.

General audience of December 18, 1996

Christ Calls Women
to Share His Mission

The words of the aged Simeon, announcing to Mary her sharing in the Messiah's saving mission, shed light on woman's role in the mystery of redemption. Indeed, Mary is not only an individual person, but she is also the Daughter of Zion, the new woman standing at the Redeemer's side in order to share his passion and to give birth in the Spirit to the children of God. This reality is expressed by the popular depiction of the "seven swords" that pierce Mary's heart. This image highlights the deep link between the mother, who is identified with the Daughter of Zion and with the Church, and the sorrowful destiny of the incarnate Word.

Giving back her Son, whom she had just received from God, to consecrate him for his saving mission, Mary also gave herself to this mission. It was an act of interior sharing that is not only the fruit of natural maternal affection, but above all expressed the consent of the new woman to Christ's redemptive work.

In his words Simeon indicated the purpose of Jesus' sacrifice and Mary's suffering: these would come about so "that thoughts out of many hearts may be revealed" (Lk 2:35). Jesus, "a sign that will be opposed" (Lk 2:34), who involves his mother in his suffering, will lead men and women to take a stand in his regard, inviting them to make a fundamental decision. He "is set for the fall and rising of many in Israel" (Lk 2:34).

Thus Mary was united to her divine Son in this "contradiction," in view of the work of salvation. Certainly there is a risk of ruin for those who reject Christ, but the resurrection of many is a marvelous effect of the redemption. This proclamation alone kindles great hope in the hearts of those to whom the fruit of the sacrifice already bears witness. Directing the Blessed Virgin's attention to these prospects of salvation before the ritual offering, Simeon seemed to suggest to Mary that she perform this act as a contribution to humanity's ransom. Simeon did not speak to Joseph or about Joseph; his words were addressed to Mary, whom he associated with the destiny of her Son.

The chronological priority of Mary's action does not obscure Jesus' primacy. In describing Mary's role in the economy of salvation, the Second Vatican Council recalled that "she devoted herself totally as a handmaid of the Lord to the person and work of her Son, under him and with him, by the grace of almighty God, serving the mystery of redemption" (*LG* 56). At the presentation of Jesus in the Temple, Mary served the mystery of redemption under Christ and with Christ; he has the principal role in salvation and must be ransomed by a ritual offering. Mary was joined to the sacrifice of her Son by the sword that will pierce her soul.

The primacy of Christ does not rule out but supports and demands the proper, irreplaceable role of woman. By involving his mother in his own sacrifice, Christ wants to reveal its deep human roots and to show us an anticipation of the priestly offering of the cross. The divine intention to call for the specific involvement of woman in the work of redemption can be seen by the fact that Simeon's prophecy was addressed to Mary alone, although Joseph also took part in the offering rite.

The conclusion of the episode of Jesus' presentation in the Temple seems to confirm the meaning and value of the feminine presence in the economy of salvation. The meeting with a woman, Anna, brings to a close these special moments when the Old Testament as it were was handed over to the New.

Like Simeon, this woman had no special status among the Chosen People, but her life seems to have a lofty value in God's eyes. St. Luke calls her a "prophetess," probably because many consulted her for her gift of discernment and the holy life she led under the inspiration of the Spirit of the Lord. Anna was advanced in age, being 84 years old, and had long been a widow. Totally consecrated to God, "she never left the Temple, serving God day and night with fasting and prayer" (Lk 2:37). She represents those who, having intensely lived in expectation of the Messiah, are able to accept the fulfillment of the promise with joyous exultation. The evangelist mentions that "coming up at that very hour she gave thanks to God" (2:38).

Staying constantly in the Temple, she could, perhaps more easily than Simeon, meet Jesus at the end of a life dedicated to the Lord and enriched by listening to the Word and by prayer. At the dawn of redemption, we can glimpse in the prophetess Anna all women who, with holiness of life and in prayerful expectation, are ready to accept Christ's presence and to praise God every day for the marvels wrought by his everlasting mercy.

Chosen to meet the child, Simeon and Anna had a deep experience of sharing the joy of Jesus' presence with Mary and Joseph and spreading it where they live. Anna in particular shows wonderful zeal in speaking about Jesus, thus witnessing to her simple and generous faith. This faith prepared others to accept the Messiah in their lives.

Luke's expression, "she...spoke of him to all who were looking for the redemption of Jerusalem" (2:38), seems to credit her as a symbol of the women who, dedicated to spreading the Gospel, will arouse and nourish the hope of salvation.

General audience of January 8, 1997

Mary Cooperated
By Personal Obedience

The evangelist Luke describes the young Jesus' pilgrimage to the Temple in Jerusalem as the last episode of the infancy narrative, before the start of John the Baptist's preaching. It was a usual occasion which sheds light on the long years of his hidden life in Nazareth. On this occasion, with his strong personality Jesus revealed that he was aware of his mission. He gave to this second "entry" into his "Father's house" the meaning of his total gift of self to God which had already marked his presentation in the Temple.

This passage seems to contrast with Luke's note that Jesus was obedient to Joseph and Mary (cf. 2:51). But if one looks closely, here Jesus seemed to put himself in a conscious and almost deliberate antithesis to his normal state as son, unexpectedly causing a definite separation from Mary and Joseph. As his rule of conduct, Jesus stated that he belongs only to the Father and did not mention the ties to his earthly family.

Through this episode, Jesus prepared his Mother for the mystery of the redemption. During those three dramatic days when the Son withdrew from them to stay in the Temple, Mary and Joseph experienced an anticipation of the Triduum of Jesus' passion, death and resurrection. Letting his Mother and Joseph depart for Galilee without telling them of his intention to stay behind in Jerusalem, Jesus brought them into the mystery of that suffering which leads to joy, anticipating what he would later accomplish with his disciples through the announcement of his Passover.

According to Luke's account, after a day's traveling on the return journey to Nazareth, Mary and Joseph were worried and anguished over the fate of the child Jesus. They looked for him in vain among their relatives and acquaintances. Returning to Jerusalem and finding him in the Temple, they were astonished to see him "sitting among the teachers, listening to them and asking them questions" (Lk 2:46). His behavior seems most unusual. Certainly for his parents, finding him on the third day meant discovering another aspect of his person and his mission.

He took the role of teacher, as he would later do in his public life, speaking words that aroused admiration: "All who heard him were astounded at his understanding and his answers" (2:47). Revealing a wisdom that amazed his listeners, he began to practice the art of dialogue that would be a characteristic of his saving mission. His Mother asked Jesus: "Son, why have you treated us so? Behold, your father and I have been looking for you anxiously" (Lk 2:48). Here we can discern an echo of the "whys" asked by so many mothers about the suffering their children cause them, as well as the questions welling up in the heart of every man and woman in times of trial.

In the form of a question, Jesus' reply is highly significant: "How is it that you sought me? Did you not know that I must be in my Father's house?" (Lk 2:49). With this response, he disclosed the mystery of his person to Mary and Joseph in an unexpected, unforeseen way, inviting them to go beyond appearances and unfolding before them new horizons for his future. In his reply to his anguished Mother, the Son immediately revealed the reason for his behavior. Mary had said:

"Your father," indicating Joseph; Jesus replied: "My Father," meaning the heavenly Father.

Referring to his divine origin, he did not so much want to state that the Temple, his Father's house, is the natural "place" for his presence, as that he must be concerned about all that regards his Father and his plan. He meant to stress that his Father's will is the only norm requiring his obedience.

This reference to his total dedication to God's plan is highlighted in the Gospel text by the words: "I must be," which will later appear in his prediction of the passion (cf. Mk 8:31). His parents then are asked to let him go and carry out his mission wherever the heavenly Father will lead him.

The evangelist comments: "They did not understand the saying which he spoke to them" (Lk 2:50). Mary and Joseph did not perceive the sense of Jesus' answer, nor the way (apparently a rejection) he reacted to their parental concern. With this attitude, Jesus intended to reveal the mysterious aspects of his intimacy with the Father, aspects which Mary intuited without knowing how to associate them with the trial she was undergoing.

Luke's words teach us how Mary lived in the depths of her being this truly unusual episode. She "kept all these things in her heart" (Lk 2:51). The Mother of Jesus associated these events with the mystery of her Son, revealed to her at the annunciation. She pondered them in the silence of contemplation, offering her cooperation in the spirit of a renewed "fiat." In this way the first link was forged in a chain of events that would gradually lead Mary beyond the natural role deriving from her motherhood, to put herself at the service of her divine Son's mission.

At the Temple in Jerusalem, in this prelude to his saving mission, Jesus associated his Mother with himself. No longer was she merely the one who gave him birth, but the woman who through her own obedience to the Father's plan can cooperate in the mystery of redemption. Thus keeping in her heart an event so charged with meaning, Mary attained a new dimension of her cooperation in salvation.

General audience of January 15, 1997

Mary's "Hidden Life" Is an Example to Mothers

The Gospels offer very sparse information about the years the holy family spent in Nazareth. St. Matthew tells us that after the return from Egypt, Joseph decided to make Nazareth the holy family's permanent home (cf. Mt 2:22–23), but then gives no further information except that Joseph was a carpenter (Mt 13:55). For his part, St. Luke twice mentions the holy family's return to Nazareth (cf. Lk 2:39, 51) and gives two brief references to the years of Jesus' childhood, before and after the episode of the pilgrimage to Jerusalem: "The child grew and became strong, filled with wisdom, and the favor of God was upon him" (Lk 2:40), and "Jesus increased in wisdom, age and grace before God and men" (Lk 2:52).

In relating these brief remarks about Jesus' life, Luke is probably referring to Mary's memories of a period of profound intimacy with her Son. The union between Jesus and the one who was "full of grace" goes far beyond what normally exists between mother and child, because it is rooted in a particular supernatural condition and reinforced by the special conformity of both to the divine will. Thus we can conclude that the atmosphere of tranquillity and peace in the house of Nazareth and their constant seeking to fulfill God's plan gave an extraordinary and unique depth to the union of mother and son.

Mary's awareness that she was carrying out a task God entrusted to her gave a higher meaning to her daily life. The simple, humble chores of everyday life took on special value in her eyes, since she performed them as a service to Christ's mission.

Mary's example enlightens and encourages the experience of so many women who carry out their daily tasks exclusively in the home. It is a question of a humble, hidden, repetitive effort, and is often not sufficiently appreciated. Nonetheless, the long years Mary spent in the house of Nazareth reveal the enormous potential of genuine love and thus of salvation. The simplicity of the lives of so many housewives, seen as a mission of service and love, is of extraordinary value in the Lord's eyes.

One can certainly say that for Mary life in Nazareth was not dominated by monotony. In her contact with the growing Jesus, she strove to penetrate the mystery of her Son through contemplation and adoration. St. Luke says: "Mary kept all these things, pondering them in her heart" (Lk 2:19; cf. 2:51). "All these things": they are the events in which she was both participant and spectator, starting with the annunciation, but above all, it is the life of her child. Every day of intimacy with him was an invitation to know him better, to discover more deeply the meaning of his presence and the mystery of his person.

Someone might think that it was easy for Mary to believe, living as she did in daily contact with Jesus. In this regard, however, we must remember that the unique aspects of her Son's personality were usually hidden. Even if his way of acting was exemplary, he lived a life similar to that of his peers. During his thirty years of life in Nazareth, Jesus did not reveal his supernatural qualities and worked no miracles. At the first extraordinary manifestations of his personality, associated with the beginning of his preaching, his relatives (called "brothers" in the Gospel), assumed—according to one interpretation—responsibility for taking him home, because they felt his behavior was not normal (cf. Mk 3:21).

In the dignified and hard-working atmosphere of Nazareth, Mary strove to understand the workings of Providence in her Son's mission. In this regard, a subject of particular reflection for his Mother was certainly the statement Jesus made in the Temple of Jerusalem when he was twelve years old: "Did you not know that I must be in my Father's house?" (Lk 2:49). Meditating on this, Mary could better understand the meaning of Jesus' divine sonship and her own motherhood, as she endeavored to discern in her Son's conduct the traits revealing his likeness to the one he called "my Father."

Communion of life with Jesus in the house of Nazareth led Mary not only to advance "in her pilgrimage of faith" (*LG* 58), but also in hope. This virtue, cultivated and sustained by her memory of the annunciation and of Simeon's words, embraced the whole span of her earthly life. But she practiced it especially during the thirty years of silence and hiddenness spent in Nazareth.

At home, the Blessed Virgin experienced hope in its highest form. She knew she would not be disappointed even if she did not know the times or the ways in which God would fulfill his promise. In the darkness of faith and in the absence of extraordinary signs announcing the beginning of her Son's messianic task, she hoped beyond all evidence, awaiting the fulfillment of God's promise. A setting for growth in faith and hope, the house of Nazareth became a place of lofty witness to charity. The love that Christ wanted to pour forth in the world was kindled and burned first of all in his Mother's heart. It was precisely in the home that the proclamation of the Gospel of divine love was prepared. Looking at Nazareth, contemplating the mystery of the hidden life of Jesus and the Blessed Virgin, we are invited to reflect on the mystery of our life which—St.

Paul recalls —"is hidden with Christ in God" (Col 3:3). It is often a life that seems humble and obscure in the world's eyes, but which, following Mary's example, can reveal unexpected possibilities of salvation, radiating the love and peace of Christ.

General audience of January 29, 1997

Jesus Worked a Miracle at Mary's Request

In the episode of the wedding at Cana, St. John presents Mary's first intervention in the public life of Jesus and highlights her cooperation in her Son's mission. At the beginning of the account the evangelist tells us that "the Mother of Jesus was there" (Jn 2:1). As if to suggest that her presence was the reason for the couple's invitation to Jesus and his disciples (cf. *RM* 21), he adds "Jesus also was invited to the marriage, with his disciples" (Jn 2:2). With these remarks, John seems to indicate that at Cana, as in the fundamental event of the Incarnation, it was Mary who introduced the Savior.

The meaning and role of the Blessed Virgin's presence became evident when the wine ran out. As a skilled and wise housewife, she immediately noticed and intervened so that no one's joy was marred and, above all, to help the newly married couple in difficulty. Turning to Jesus with the words: "They have no wine" (Jn 2:3), Mary expressed her concern to him about this situation, expecting him to solve it. More precisely, according to some exegetes, his Mother was expecting an extraordinary sign, since Jesus had no wine at his disposal.

The choice made by Mary, who could perhaps have obtained the necessary wine elsewhere, shows the courage of her faith, because until that moment Jesus had worked no miracles, either in Nazareth or in his public life. At Cana, the Blessed Virgin once again showed her total availability to God. At the annunciation she had contributed to the miracle of the virginal conception by believing in Jesus before seeing him; here, her trust in Jesus' as yet unrevealed power caused him to perform his "first sign," the miraculous transformation of water into wine. In that way she preceded in faith the disciples who, as John says, would believe after the miracle: Jesus "manifested his glory, and his disciples believed in him" (Jn 2:11). Thus, Mary strengthened their faith by obtaining this miraculous sign.

Jesus' answer to Mary's words, "O woman, what have you to do with me? My hour has not yet come" (Jn 2:4), appears to express a refusal, as if putting his Mother's faith to the test. According to one interpretation, from the moment his mission began Jesus seemed to call into question the natural relationship of son to which his mother referred. The sentence, in the local parlance, was meant to stress a distance between the persons, by excluding a communion of life. This distance did not preclude respect and esteem. The term "woman" by which he addressed his Mother was used with a nuance that would recur in the conversations with the Canaanite woman (cf. Mt 15:28), the Samaritan woman (cf. Jn 4:21), the adulteress (cf. Jn 8:10) and Mary Magdalene (cf. Jn 20:13), in contexts that show Jesus' positive relationship with his female interlocutors. With the expression: "O woman, what have you to do with me?" Jesus intended to put Mary's cooperation on the level of salvation which, by involving her faith and hope, required her to go beyond her natural role of mother.

Of much greater import is the reason Jesus gives: "My hour has not yet come" (Jn 2:4).

Some scholars who have studied this sacred text, following St. Augustine's interpretation, identify this "hour" with the passion event. For others, instead, it refers to the first miracle in which the prophet of Nazareth's messianic power would be revealed. Yet others hold that the sentence is interrogative and an extension of the question that precedes it: "What have you to do with me? Has my hour not yet come?" Jesus gave Mary to understand that henceforth he no longer depended on her, but had to take the initiative for doing his Father's work. Then Mary docilely refrained from insisting with him and instead turned to the servants, telling them to obey him.

In any case her trust in her Son was rewarded. She left Jesus totally free to act, and he worked the miracle, recognizing his Mother's courage and docility: "Jesus said to them, 'Fill the jars with water.' And they filled them up to the brim" (Jn 2:7). Thus their obedience also helped to procure wine in abundance.

Mary's request: "Do whatever he tells you," keeps its ever timely value for Christians of every age and is destined to renew its marvelous effect in everyone's life. It is an exhortation to trust without hesitation, especially when one does not understand the meaning or benefit of what Christ asks.

As in the account of the Canaanite woman (Mt 15:24–26), Jesus' apparent refusal exalts the woman's faith. Jesus' words, "My hour has not yet come," together with the working of the first miracle, demonstrate Mary's great faith and the power of her prayer. The episode of the wedding at Cana urges us to be courageous in faith and to experience in our lives the truth of the Gospel words: "Ask and it will be given you" (Mt 7:7; Lk 11:9).

General audience of February 26, 1997

Mary Was Active in Her Son's Mission

Describing Mary's presence in Jesus' public life, the Second Vatican Council recalled her involvement at Cana on the occasion of the first miracle: "At the marriage feast of Cana, moved with pity, she brought about by her intercession the beginning of miracles of Jesus the Messiah (cf. Jn 2:1–11)" (*LG* 58). Following the evangelist John, the Council pointed out the Mother's discreet and effective role, when by her words she persuaded her Son to perform his "first sign." Although her influence was discreet and maternal, her presence proved decisive.

The Blessed Virgin's initiative is all the more surprising if one considers the inferior status of women in Jewish society. At Cana, Jesus not only recognized the dignity and role of the feminine genius, but by welcoming his Mother's intervention, he gave her the opportunity to participate in his messianic work. The epithet "woman," which Jesus used to address Mary (cf. Jn 2:4), is not in contrast with his intention. It has no negative connotations, and Jesus used it again when he addressed his Mother at the foot of the cross (cf. Jn 19:26). According to some interpretations, this title "woman" presents Mary as the New Eve, the mother in faith of all believers.

In the text cited, the Council used the expression "moved with pity," letting it be understood that Mary was prompted by her merciful heart. Having sensed the eventual disappointment of the newly married couple and guests because of the lack of wine, the Blessed Virgin compassionately suggested to Jesus that he intervene with his messianic power.

To some, Mary's request may appear excessive, since it subordinates the beginning of the Messiah's miracles to an act of filial devotion. Jesus himself dealt with this difficulty when, by assenting to his mother's request, he showed the Lord's superabundance in responding to human expectations, manifesting also what a mother's love can do.

The expression "the beginning of his miracles," which the Council took from John's text, attracts our attention. In the Prologue of his Gospel John uses the Greek term *arche,* translated as "beginning": "In the beginning was the Word" (1:1). This significant coincidence suggests a parallel between the origins of Christ's glory in eternity and the first manifestation of this same glory in his earthly mission.

By emphasizing Mary's initiative in the first miracle and then recalling her presence on Calvary at the foot of the cross, the evangelist helps us understand how Mary's cooperation is extended to the whole of Christ's work. The Blessed Virgin's request is placed within the divine plan of salvation.

In the first "sign" Jesus performed, the Fathers of the Church glimpsed an important symbolic dimension, seeing the transformation of the water into wine as the announcement of the passage from the Old to the New Covenant. At Cana it was precisely the water in the jars, destined for the purification of the Jews and the fulfillment of the legal prescriptions (cf. Mk 7:1–15), which became the new wine of the wedding feast, a symbol of the definitive union between God and humanity.

The context of a wedding banquet, which Jesus chose for his first miracle, refers to the marriage symbolism used frequently in the Old Testament to indicate the covenant between God and his people (cf. Hos 2:21; Jer 2:1–8; Ps 44, etc.), and in the New Testament to signify Christ's union with the Church (cf. Jn 3:28–30; Eph 5:25–32; Rv 21:1–2, etc.). Jesus' presence at Cana is also a sign of God's saving plan for marriage. In this perspective, the lack of wine can be interpreted as an allusion to the lack of love that unfortunately often threatens marital unions. Mary asks Jesus to intervene on behalf of all married couples, who can only be freed from the dangers of infidelity, misunderstanding and division by a love which is based on God. The grace of the sacrament offers the couple this superior strength of love, which can reinforce their commitment to fidelity even in difficult circumstances.

According to the interpretation of Christian authors, the miracle at Cana also has a deep Eucharistic meaning. Jesus performed this miracle near the time of the Jewish feast of Passover (cf. Jn 2:13), as he did in multiplying the loaves (cf. Jn 6:4). He thus showed his intention to prepare the true paschal banquet, the Eucharist. His desire at the wedding in Cana seems to be emphasized further by the presence of wine, which alludes to the blood of the New Covenant, and by the context of a banquet. In this way, after being the reason for Jesus' presence at the celebration, Mary obtained the miracle of the new wine which prefigures the Eucharist, the supreme sign of the presence of her risen Son among the disciples.

At the end of the account of Jesus' first miracle, made possible by the firm faith of the Lord's Mother in her divine Son, the evangelist John concludes: "and his disciples believed in him" (2:11). At Cana, Mary began the Church's journey of faith, preceding the disciples and directing the servants' attention to Christ. Her persevering intercession likewise encourages those who at times face the experience of "God's silence." They are asked to hope beyond all hope, always trusting in the Lord's goodness.

General audience of March 5, 1997

Mary Had a Role in Jesus' Public Ministry

After recalling Mary's intervention at the wedding feast of Cana, the Second Vatican Council emphasized her participation in the public life of Jesus: "In the course of her Son's preaching she received the words whereby, in extolling a kingdom beyond the calculations and bonds of flesh and blood, he declared blessed (cf. Mk 3:35, par.; Lk 11:27–28) those who heard and kept the Word of God, as she was faithfully doing (cf. Lk 2:19, 51)" (*LG* 58).

The beginning of Jesus' mission also meant separation from his Mother, who did not always follow her son in his travels on the roads of Palestine. Jesus deliberately chose separation from his Mother and from family affection, as can be inferred from the conditions he gave his disciples for following him and for dedicating themselves to proclaiming God's kingdom.

Nevertheless, Mary sometimes heard her Son's preaching. We can assume that she was present in the synagogue of Nazareth when Jesus, after reading Isaiah's prophecy, commented on the text and applied it to himself (cf. Lk 4:18–30). How much she must have suffered on that occasion, after sharing the general amazement at "the gracious words which preceded out of his mouth" (Lk 4:22), as she observed the harsh hostility of her fellow citizens who drove Jesus from the synagogue and even tried to kill him! The drama of that moment is evident in the words of the Evangelist Luke: "They rose up and put him out of the city and led him to the brow of the hill on which their city was built, that they might throw him down headlong. But passing through the midst of them he went away" (4:29–30). Realizing after this event that there would be other trials, Mary confirmed and deepened her total obedience to the Father's will, offering him her loneliness and her suffering as a mother.

According to the Gospels, Mary had the opportunity to hear her Son on other occasions as well, first at Capernaum, where Jesus went after the wedding feast of Cana, "with his mother and his brethren and his disciples" (Jn 2:12). For the Passover, moreover, she was probably able to follow him to the Temple in Jerusalem, which Jesus called his Father's house and for which he was consumed with zeal (cf. Jn 2:16–17). Finding herself later among the crowd and not being able to approach Jesus, she heard him replying to those who had told him that she and their relatives had arrived: "My mother and my brethren are those who hear the Word of God and do it" (Lk 8:21). With these words, Christ, although relativizing family ties, is addressing great praise to his Mother by affirming a far loftier bond with her. Indeed, in listening to her Son, Mary accepted all his words and faithfully put them into practice.

We can imagine that, although she did not follow Jesus on his missionary journey, she was informed of her Son's apostolic activities, lovingly and anxiously receiving news of his preaching from the lips of those who had met him. Separation did not mean distance of heart, nor did it prevent the Mother from spiritually following her Son, from keeping and meditating on his teaching as she had done during Jesus' hidden life in Nazareth. Her faith enabled her to grasp the meaning of Jesus' words before and better than his disciples, who often did not understand his teaching, especially the references to his future passion (cf. Mt 16:21–23; Mk 9:32; Lk 9:45).

Following the events in her Son's life, Mary shared in his drama of experiencing rejection from some of the Chosen People. This rejection first appeared during his visit to Nazareth and became more and more obvious in the words and attitudes of the leaders of the people. In this way the Blessed Virgin would often have come to know the criticism, insults and threats directed at Jesus. In Nazareth too she would have frequently been troubled by disbelief of relatives and acquaintances who would try to use Jesus (cf. Jn 7:2–5) or to stop his mission (Mk 3:21). Through this suffering borne with great dignity and hiddenness, Mary shared the journey of her Son "to Jerusalem" (Lk 9:51). More and more closely united with him in faith, hope and love, she cooperated in salvation.

The Blessed Virgin thus becomes a model for those who accept Christ's words. Believing in the divine message since the annunciation and fully supporting the Person of the Son, she teaches us to listen to the Savior with trust, to discover in him the divine Word who transforms and renews our life. Her experience also encourages us to accept the trials and suffering that come from fidelity to Christ, keeping our gaze fixed on the happiness Jesus promised those who listen to him and keep his word.

General audience of March 12, 1997

Mary United Herself to Jesus' Offering

Regina caeli, laetare, alleluia!

So the Church sings in the Easter season, inviting the faithful to join in the spiritual joy of Mary, Mother of the Redeemer. The Blessed Virgin's gladness at Christ's resurrection is even greater if one considers her intimate participation in Jesus' entire life. In accepting with complete availability the words of the angel Gabriel, who announced to her that she would become the Mother of the Messiah, Mary began her participation in the drama of redemption. Her involvement in her Son's sacrifice, revealed by Simeon during the presentation in the Temple, continued not only in the episode of the losing and finding of the twelve-year-old Jesus, but also throughout his public life.

However, the Blessed Virgin's association with Christ's mission reached its culmination in Jerusalem, at the time of the Redeemer's passion and death. As the fourth Gospel testifies, she was in the Holy City at the time, probably for the celebration of the Jewish feast of Passover. The Council stressed the profound dimension of the Blessed Virgin's presence on Calvary, recalling that she "faithfully persevered in her union with her Son unto the cross" (*LG* 58), and points out that this union "in the work of salvation is made manifest from the time of Christ's virginal conception up to his death" (*LG* 57).

With our gaze illumined by the radiance of the resurrection, we pause to reflect on the Mother's involvement in her Son's redeeming passion, which was completed by her sharing in his suffering. Let us return again, but now in the perspective of the resurrection, to the foot of the cross where the Mother "stood, in keeping with the divine plan (cf. Jn 19:25), grieving exceedingly with her only begotten Son, uniting herself with a maternal heart with his sacrifice, and lovingly consenting to the immolation of this victim which she herself had brought forth" (*LG* 58).

With these words, the Council reminded us of "Mary's compassion." In her heart reverberated all that Jesus suffered in body and soul. The Council thus emphasized Mary's willingness to share in her Son's redeeming sacrifice and to join her own maternal suffering to his priestly offering. The Council text also stresses that her consent to Jesus' immolation was not passive acceptance but a genuine act of love, by which she offered her Son as a "victim" of expiation for the sins of all humanity.

Lastly, *Lumen Gentium* relates the Blessed Virgin to Christ, who has the lead role in redemption, making it clear that in associating herself "with his sacrifice" she remains subordinate to her divine Son.

In the fourth Gospel, St. John says that "standing by the cross of Jesus were his mother and his mother's sister, Mary the wife of Clopas and Mary Magdalene" (19:25). By using the verb "to stand," which literally means "to be on one's feet," "to stand erect," perhaps the evangelist intends to present the dignity and strength which Mary and the other women showed in their sorrow. The Blessed Virgin's "standing erect" at the foot of the cross recalls her unfailing constancy and extraordinary courage in facing suffering. In the tragic events of Calvary, Mary was sustained by faith, strengthened during the events of her life and especially during Jesus' public life. The Council recalled that "the Blessed Virgin advanced in her pilgrimage of faith and faithfully persevered in her union with her Son unto the cross" (*LG* 58).

Sharing his deepest feelings, she countered with forbearance and pardon the arrogant insults addressed to the crucified Messiah, associating herself with his prayer to the Father: "Forgive them, for they know not what they do" (Lk 23:34). By sharing in the feeling of abandonment to the Father's will expressed in Jesus' last words on the cross: "Father, into your hands I commend my spirit!" (Lk 23:46), she thus offered, as the Council noted, loving consent "to the immolation of this victim which she herself had brought forth" (*LG* 58).

Mary's supreme "yes" is radiant with trusting hope in the mysterious future, begun with the death of her crucified Son. The words in which Jesus taught the disciples on his way to Jerusalem "that the Son of Man must suffer many things, and be rejected by the elders and the chief priests and the scribes and be killed, and after three days rise again," reechoed in her heart at the dramatic hour of Calvary, awakening expectation of and yearning for the resurrection. Mary's hope at the foot of the cross contained a light stronger than the darkness that reigns in many hearts. In the presence of the redeeming sacrifice, the hope of the Church and of humanity was born in Mary.

General audience of April 2, 1997

Mary's Cooperation Is Totally Unique

Down the centuries the Church has reflected on Mary's cooperation in the work of salvation, deepening the analysis of her association with Christ's redemptive sacrifice. St. Augustine already gave the Blessed Virgin the title "cooperator" in the redemption (cf. *De Sancta Virginitate,* 6; *PL* 40, 399), a title which emphasizes Mary's joint but subordinate action with Christ the Redeemer.

Reflection has developed along these lines, particularly since the 15th century. Some feared there might be a desire to put Mary on the same level as Christ. Actually the Church's teaching makes a clear distinction between the Mother and the Son in the work of salvation, explaining the Blessed Virgin's subordination as cooperator to the one Redeemer. Moreover, when the Apostle Paul says: "For we are God's fellow workers" (1 Cor 3:9), he maintains the real possibility for man to cooperate with God. The collaboration of believers, which obviously excludes any equality with him, is expressed in the proclamation of the Gospel and in their personal contribution to its taking root in human hearts.

However, applied to Mary, the term "cooperator" acquires a specific meaning. The collaboration of Christians in salvation takes place after the Calvary event, whose fruits they endeavor to spread by prayer and sacrifice. Mary, instead, cooperated during the event itself and in the role of mother; thus her cooperation embraces the whole of Christ's saving work. She alone was associated in this way with the redemptive sacrifice that merited the salvation of all mankind. In union with Christ and in submission to him, she collaborated in obtaining the grace of salvation for all humanity.

The Blessed Virgin's role as cooperator has its source in her divine motherhood. By giving birth to the one who was destined to achieve man's redemption, by nourishing him, presenting him in the Temple and suffering with him as he died on the cross, "in a wholly singular way she cooperated...in the work of the Savior" (*LG* 61). Although God's call to cooperate in the work of salvation concerns every human being, the participation of the Savior's Mother in humanity's redemption is a unique and unrepeatable fact.

Despite the uniqueness of her condition, Mary is also the recipient of salvation. She is the first to be saved, redeemed by Christ "in the most sublime way" in her immaculate conception (cf. Bull *Ineffabilis Deus,* Pius IX, *Acta,* 1, 605) and filled with the grace of the Holy Spirit.

This assertion now leads to the question: what is the meaning of Mary's unique cooperation in the plan of salvation? It should be sought in God's particular intention for the Mother of the Redeemer, whom on two solemn occasions, that is, at Cana and beneath the cross, Jesus addressed as "woman" (cf. Jn 2:4; 19:26). Mary is associated as a woman in the work of salvation. Having created man "male and female" (cf. Gn 1:27), the Lord also wants to place the New Eve beside the New Adam in the redemption. Our first parents had chosen the way of sin as a couple; a new pair, the Son of God with his Mother's cooperation, would reestablish the human race in its original dignity. Mary, the New Eve, thus becomes a perfect icon of the Church. In the divine plan, at the foot of the cross, she represents redeemed humanity which, in need of salvation, is enabled to contribute to the unfolding of the saving work.

The Council had this doctrine in mind and made it its own, stressing the Blessed Virgin's contribution not only to the Redeemer's birth, but also to the life of his Mystical Body down the ages until the "eschaton." In the Church Mary "has cooperated" (cf. *LG* 63) and "cooperates" (cf. *LG* 53) in the work of salvation. In describing the mystery of the annunciation, the Council states that the Virgin of Nazareth, "embracing God's salvific will with a full heart and impeded by no sin... devoted herself totally as a handmaid of the Lord to the person and work of her Son, under him and with him, by the grace of almighty God, serving the mystery of redemption" (*LG* 56).

The Second Vatican Council, moreover, presented Mary not only as "Mother of the redeemer," but also "in a singular way [as] the generous associate," who "cooperated by her obedience, faith, hope and burning charity in the work of the Savior." The Council also recalled that the sublime fruit of this cooperation is her universal motherhood: "For this reason she is our mother in the order of grace" (*LG* 61).

We can therefore turn to the Blessed Virgin, trustfully imploring her aid in the awareness of the singular role God entrusted to her, the role of cooperator in the redemption, which she exercised throughout her life and in a special way at the foot of the cross.

General audience of April 9, 1997

To the Disciple He Said, "Behold Your Mother"

After recalling the presence of Mary and the other women at the Lord's cross, St. John relates: "When Jesus saw his mother and the disciple whom he loved standing near, he said to his mother, 'Woman, behold your son!' Then he said to the disciple, 'Behold your mother!'" (Jn 19:26–27). These particularly moving words are a "revelation scene": they reveal the deep sentiments of the dying Christ and contain a great wealth of meaning for Christian faith and spirituality. At the end of his earthly life, as he addressed his Mother and the disciple he loved, the crucified Messiah established a new relationship of love between Mary and Christians.

Interpreted at times as no more than an expression of Jesus' filial piety toward his Mother whom he entrusted for the future to his beloved disciple, these words go far beyond the contingent need to solve a family problem. Attentive consideration of the text, confirmed by the interpretation of many Fathers and by common ecclesial opinion, presents us, in Jesus' twofold entrustment, with one of the most important events for understanding the Virgin's role in the economy of salvation.

The words of the dying Jesus actually show that his first intention was not to entrust his Mother to John, but to entrust the disciple to Mary and to give her a new maternal role.

Moreover, the epithet "woman," which Jesus also used at the wedding of Cana to lead Mary to a new dimension of her existence as Mother, shows how the Savior's words are not the fruit of a simple sentiment of filial affection but are meant to be put at a higher level. Although Jesus' death caused Mary deep sorrow, it did not in itself change her normal way of life. In departing from Nazareth to start his public life, Jesus had already left his Mother alone. Moreover, the presence at the cross of her relative, Mary of Clopas, allows us to suppose that the Blessed Virgin was on good terms with her family and relatives, who could have welcomed her after her Son's death.

Instead, Jesus' words acquire their most authentic meaning in the context of his saving mission. Spoken at the moment of the redemptive sacrifice, they draw their loftiest value precisely from this sublime circumstance. After Jesus' statements to his Mother, the evangelist adds a significant clause: "Jesus, knowing that all was now finished..." (Jn 19:28), as if he wished to stress that he had brought his sacrifice to completion by entrusting his Mother to John, and in him to all men, whose Mother she became in the work of salvation.

The reality brought about by Jesus' words, that is, Mary's new motherhood in relation to the disciple, is a further sign of the great love that led Jesus to offer his life for all people. On Calvary this love was shown in the gift of a mother, his mother, who thus became our mother too. We must remember that, according to tradition, the Blessed Virgin recognized John as her son. But this privilege has been interpreted by Christians from the beginning as the sign of a spiritual generation in relation to all humanity.

The universal motherhood of Mary, the "woman" of the wedding at Cana and of Calvary, recalls Eve, "mother of all the living" (Gn 3:20). However, while the latter helped to bring sin into the world, the New Eve, Mary, cooperated in the saving event of redemption. In the Blessed Virgin the figure of "woman" is rehabilitated and her motherhood takes up the task of spreading the new life in Christ among men.

In view of this mission, the Mother was asked to make the acutely painful sacrifice of accepting her only Son's death. Jesus' words: "Woman, behold your son" enabled Mary to sense the new maternal relationship which was to extend and broaden the preceding one. Her "yes" to this plan was therefore an assent to Christ's sacrifice, which she generously accepted by complying with the divine will. Even if in God's plan Mary's motherhood was destined from the start to extend to all humanity, its universal dimension was revealed only on Calvary, by virtue of Christ's sacrifice.

Jesus' words "Behold your son" effect what they express, making Mary the mother of John and of all the disciples destined to receive the gift of divine grace. On the cross Jesus did not proclaim Mary's universal motherhood formally, but established a concrete maternal relationship between her and the beloved disciple. In the Lord's choice we can see his concern that this motherhood should not be interpreted in a vague way, but should point to Mary's intense, personal relationship with individual Christians. May each one of us, precisely through the concrete reality of Mary's universal motherhood, fully acknowledge her as our own Mother, and trustingly commend ourselves to her maternal love.

General audience of April 23, 1997

Devotion to Mary
Is Based on Jesus' Will

After entrusting John to Mary with the words "Woman, behold your son!" Jesus, from the cross, turned to his beloved disciple, saying to him, "Behold, your mother!" (Jn 19:26–27). With these words, he revealed to Mary the height of her motherhood. As mother of the Savior, she is also the mother of the redeemed, of all the members of the Mystical Body of her Son. In silence the Virgin accepted the elevation to this highest degree of her motherhood of grace, having already given a response of faith with her "yes" at the annunciation.

Jesus not only urged John to care for Mary with special love, but he entrusted her to him so that he might recognize her as his own mother. During the Last Supper, "the disciple whom Jesus loved" listened to the Master's commandment: "Love one another as I have loved you" (Jn 15:12). Leaning his head against the Lord's breast, he received from him a unique sign of love. Such experiences prepared him better to perceive in Jesus' words an invitation to accept Mary who had been given him as mother and to love her as Jesus did with filial affection. May all discover in Jesus' words: "Behold, your mother!" the invitation to accept Mary as Mother, responding to her motherly love as true children.

In the light of this entrustment to his beloved disciple, one can understand the authentic meaning of Marian devotion in the ecclesial community. It places Christians in Jesus' filial relationship to his mother, putting them in a condition to grow in intimacy with both of them. The Church's devotion to the Virgin is not only the fruit of a spontaneous response to the exceptional value of her person and the importance of her role in the work of salvation, but is based on Christ's will.

The words, "Behold, your mother!" express Jesus' intention to inspire in his disciples an attitude of love for and trust in Mary, leading them to recognize her as their mother, the mother of every believer. At the school of the Virgin, the disciples learn to know the Lord deeply, as John did, and to have an intimate and lasting relationship of love with him. They also discover the joy of entrusting themselves to the Mother's maternal love, living like affectionate and docile children.

The history of Christian piety teaches that Mary is the way which leads to Christ and that filial devotion to her takes nothing from intimacy with Jesus. Indeed, it increases it and leads to the highest levels of perfection. The countless Marian shrines throughout the world testify to the marvels wrought by grace through the intercession of Mary, Mother of the Lord and our Mother. Turning to her, drawn by her tenderness, the men and women of our time also meet Jesus, Savior and Lord of their lives. Above all, the poor, tried in heart, in their affections and in their material need find refuge and peace in the Mother of God, and discover that for all people true riches consist in the grace of conversion and of following Christ.

According to the original Greek, the gospel text continues: "From that hour the disciple took her among his possessions" (Jn 19:27). Thus, it stresses John's ready and generous adherence to Jesus' words, informing us about his behavior for his whole life as the faithful guardian and docile son of the Virgin. The hour of acceptance is that of the fulfillment of the work of salvation. Mary's spiritual motherhood and the first manifestation of the new link between her and the Lord's disciples began precisely in this context.

John took the Mother "among his possessions." These rather general words seem to highlight his initiative, full of respect and love, not only in taking Mary to his house but also in living his spiritual life in communion with her. A literal translation of the Greek expression "among his possessions" does not so much refer to material possessions since John—as St. Augustine observes (*Tract. in Ev. Ioannis,.* 119, 3)—"possessed nothing of his own," but rather to the spiritual goods or gifts received from Christ: grace (Jn 1:16), the Word (Jn 12:48; 17:8), the Spirit (Jn 7:39; 14:17), the Eucharist (Jn 6:32–58). Among these gifts which come to him from the fact that he is loved by Jesus, the disciple accepts Mary as his mother, establishing a profound communion of life with her (cf. *RM* 45, note 130). May every Christian, after the beloved disciple's example, "take Mary into his house" and make room for her in his own daily life, recognizing her providential role in the journey of salvation.

General audience of May 7, 1997

Mary Was a Witness
to the Paschal Mystery

After Jesus had been placed in the tomb, Mary "alone remained to keep alive the flame of faith, preparing to receive the joyful and astonishing announcement of the resurrection" (General Audience, April 3, 1996).* The expectation felt on Holy Saturday was one of the loftiest moments of faith for the Mother of the Lord. In the darkness that enveloped the world, she entrusted herself fully to the God of life, and thinking back to the words of her Son, she hoped in the fulfillment of the divine promises.

The Gospels mention various appearances of the risen Christ, but not a meeting between Jesus and his Mother. This silence must not lead to the conclusion that after the resurrection Christ did not appear to Mary; rather, it invites us to seek the reasons why the evangelists made such a choice.

On the supposition of an "omission," this silence could be attributed to the fact that what is necessary for our saving knowledge was entrusted to the word of those "chosen by God as witnesses" (Acts 10:41), that is, the apostles, who gave their testimony of the Lord Jesus' resurrection "with great power"

---

* This general audience, given at Easter, was not part of the series of Marian catecheses.

(cf. Acts 4:33). Before appearing to them, the risen one had appeared to several faithful women because of their ecclesial function: "Go and tell my brethren to go to Galilee, and there they will see me" (Mt 28:10). If the authors of the New Testament do not speak of the Mother's encounter with her risen Son, this can perhaps be attributed to the fact that such a witness would have been considered too biased by those who denied the Lord's resurrection and therefore not worthy of belief.

Furthermore, the Gospels report a small number of appearances by the risen Jesus and certainly not a complete summary of all that happened during the forty days after Easter. St. Paul recalls that he appeared "to more than 500 brethren at one time" (1 Cor 15:6). How do we explain the fact that an exceptional event known to so many is not mentioned by the evangelists? It is an obvious sign that other appearances of the risen one were not recorded, although they were among the well-known events that occurred.

How could the Blessed Virgin, present in the first community of disciples (cf. Acts 1:14), be excluded from those who met her divine Son after he had risen from the dead? It is legitimate to think that the Mother was probably the first person to whom the risen Jesus appeared. Could not Mary's absence from the group of women who went to the tomb at dawn (cf. Mk 16:1; Mt 28:1) indicate that she had already met Jesus? This inference would also be confirmed by the fact that the first witnesses of the resurrection, by Jesus' will, were the women who had remained faithful at the foot of the cross and therefore were more steadfast in faith. The risen one entrusted to one of them, Mary Magdalene, the message to be passed on to the apostles (cf. Jn 20:17–18). Perhaps this fact, too, allows us to think that Jesus showed himself first to his mother, who had been the most faithful and had kept her faith intact when put to the test.

Lastly, the unique and special character of the Blessed Virgin's presence at Calvary and her perfect union with the Son in his suffering on the cross seem to postulate a very particular sharing on her part in the mystery of the resurrection. A fifth-century author, Sedulius, maintained that in the splendor of his risen life Christ first showed himself to his mother. She who at the annunciation was the way he entered the world, was called to spread the marvelous news of the resurrection in order to become the herald of his glorious coming. Thus, bathed in the glory of the risen one, she anticipated the Church's splendor (cf. Sedulius, *Paschale Carmen,* 5, 357–364, *CSEL* 10, 140 f.).

It seems reasonable to think that Mary, as the image and model of the Church which waits for the risen one and meets him in the group of disciples during his Easter appearances, had had a personal contact with her risen Son, so that she too could delight in the fullness of paschal joy.

Present at Calvary on Good Friday (cf. Jn 19:25) and in the upper room on Pentecost (cf. Acts 1:14), the Blessed Virgin too was probably a privileged witness of Christ's resurrection, completing in this way her participation in all the essential moments of the Paschal Mystery. Welcoming the risen Jesus, Mary is also a sign and an anticipation of humanity, which hopes to achieve its fulfillment through the resurrection of the dead.

In the Easter season, the Christian community addresses the Mother of the Lord and invites her to rejoice: *Regina caeli, laetare, alleluia!* "Queen of heaven rejoice, alleluia!" Thus it recalls Mary's joy at Jesus' resurrection, prolonging in time the "rejoice" that the angel addressed to her at the annunciation, so that she might become a cause of "great joy" for all people.

General audience of May 21, 1997

Mary Prays for the Outpouring of the Spirit

Retracing the course of the Virgin Mary's life, the Second Vatican Council recalled her presence in the community waiting for Pentecost: "But since it has pleased God not to manifest solemnly the mystery of the salvation of the human race before he would pour forth the Spirit promised by Christ, we see the apostles before the day of Pentecost 'persevering with one mind in prayer with the women and Mary, the Mother of Jesus, and with his brethren' (Acts 1:14), and Mary by her prayers imploring the gift of the Spirit, who had already overshadowed her in the annunciation" (*LG* 59). The first community was the prelude to the birth of the Church. The Blessed Virgin's presence helps to sketch her definitive features, a fruit of the gift of Pentecost.

In the atmosphere of expectation that prevailed in the upper room after the ascension, what was Mary's position in relation to the descent of the Holy Spirit? The Council expressly underscored her prayerful presence while waiting for the outpouring of the Paraclete: she prayed, "imploring the gift of the Spirit." This observation is especially significant since at the annunciation the Holy Spirit had descended upon her, "overshadowing" her and bringing about the Incarnation of the Word.

Having already had a unique experience of the effectiveness of such a gift, the Blessed Virgin was in a condition to appreciate it more than anyone. Indeed, she owed her motherhood to the mysterious intervention of the Spirit, who had made her the way by which the Savior came into the world.

Unlike those in the upper room who were waiting in fearful expectation she, fully aware of the importance of her Son's promise to the disciples (cf. Jn 14:16), helped the community to be well disposed to the coming of the "Paraclete." Thus, while her unique experience made her ardently long for the Spirit's coming, it also involved her in preparing the minds and heart of those around her.

During that prayer in the upper room, in an attitude of deep communion with the apostles, with some women and with Jesus' "brethren," the Mother of the Lord prayed for the community. It was appropriate that the first outpouring of the Spirit upon her, which had happened in view of her divine motherhood, should be repeated and reinforced. At the foot of the cross Mary was entrusted with a new motherhood, which concerned Jesus' disciples. This mission demanded a renewed gift of the Spirit. The Blessed Virgin, therefore, wanted it for the fruitfulness of her spiritual motherhood.

While at the moment of the Incarnation the Holy Spirit had descended upon her as a person called to take part worthily in the great mystery, everything was now accomplished for the sake of the Church, whose image, model and mother Mary is called to be. In the Church and for the Church, mindful of Jesus' promise, she waited for Pentecost and implored a multiplicity of gifts for everyone, in accordance with each one's personality and mission.

Mary's prayer has particular significance in the Christian community. It fosters the coming of the Spirit, imploring his action in the hearts of the disciples and in the world. Just as in the Incarnation the Spirit had formed the physical body of

Christ in her virginal womb, in the upper room the same Spirit came down to give life to the Mystical Body. Thus, Pentecost is also a fruit of the Blessed Virgin's incessant prayer, which is accepted by the Paraclete with special favor because it is an expression of her motherly love for the Lord's disciples.

In contemplating Mary's powerful intercession as she waited for the Holy Spirit, Christians of every age have frequently had recourse to her intercession on the long and tiring journey to salvation, in order to receive the gifts of the Paraclete in greater abundance.

Responding to the prayer of the Blessed Virgin and the community gathered in the upper room on the day of Pentecost, the Holy Spirit bestowed the fullness of his gifts on the Blessed Virgin and those present, working a deep transformation in them for the sake of spreading the Good News. The Mother of Christ and his disciples were granted new strength and new apostolic energy for the Church's growth. In particular, the outpouring of the Spirit led Mary to exercise her spiritual motherhood in an exceptional way, through her presence imbued with charity and her witness of faith.

In the nascent Church she passed on to the disciples her memories of the Incarnation, the infancy, the hidden life and the mission of her divine Son as a priceless treasure, thus helping to make him known and to strengthen the faith of believers. We have no information about Mary's activity in the early Church, but we may suppose that after Pentecost her life would have continued to be hidden and discreet, watchful and effective. Since she was enlightened and guided by the Spirit, she exercised a deep influence on the community of the Lord's disciples.

General audience of May 28, 1997

Mary and the Human Drama of Death

Concerning the end of Mary's earthly life, the Council used the terms of the Bull defining the dogma of the assumption and stated: "The immaculate Virgin, preserved free from all guilt of original sin, on the completion of her earthly sojourn was taken up body and soul into heavenly glory" (*LG* 59). With this formula, following my venerable Predecessor Pius XII, *Lumen Gentium* made no pronouncement on the question of Mary's death. Nevertheless, Pius XII did not intend to deny the fact of her death, but merely did not judge it opportune to affirm solemnly the death of the Mother of God as a truth to be accepted by all believers.

Some theologians have maintained that the Blessed Virgin did not die and was immediately raised from earthly life to heavenly glory. However, this opinion was unknown until the 17th century, whereas a common tradition actually exists which sees Mary's death as her entry into heavenly glory. Could Mary of Nazareth have experienced the drama of death in her own flesh? Reflecting on Mary's destiny and her relationship with her divine Son, it seems legitimate to answer in the affirmative. Since Christ died, it would be difficult to maintain the contrary for his Mother.

The Fathers of the Church, who had no doubts in this

regard, reasoned along these lines. One need only quote St. Jacob of Sarug (d. 521), who wrote that when the time came for Mary "to walk on the way of all generations," that is, the way of death, "the group of the twelve apostles" gathered to bury "the virginal body of the Blessed One" (*Discourse on the Burial of the Holy Mother of God,* 87–99 in C. Vona, *Lateranum* 19 [1953], 188).

St. Modestus of Jerusalem (d. 634), after a lengthy discussion of "the most blessed dormition of the most glorious Mother of God," ends his eulogy by exalting the miraculous intervention of Christ who "raised her from the tomb," to take her up with him in glory (*Enc. in dormitionem Deiparae semperque Virginis Mariae,* nn. 7 and 14: *PG* 86 *bis,* 3293; 3311). St. John Damascene (d. 704) for his part asks: "Why is it that she who in giving birth surpassed all the limits of nature should now bend to its laws and her immaculate body be subjected to death?" He answers: "To be clothed in immortality, it is of course necessary that the mortal part be shed, since even the master of nature did not refuse the experience of death. Indeed, he died according to the flesh and by dying destroyed death; on corruption he bestowed incorruption and made death the source of resurrection" (*Panegyric on the Dormition of the Mother of God,* n. 10: *SC* 80, 107).

It is true that in revelation death is presented as a punishment for sin. However, the fact that the Church proclaims Mary free from original sin by a unique divine privilege does not lead to the conclusion that she also received physical immortality. The Mother is not superior to the Son who underwent death, giving it a new meaning and changing it into a means of salvation.

Involved in Christ's redemptive work and associated in his saving sacrifice, Mary was able to share in his suffering and death for the sake of humanity's redemption. What Severus of Antioch says about Christ also applies to her: "Without a preliminary death, how could the resurrection have taken place?"

(*Antijulianistica,* Beirut, 1931, 194 f.). To share in Christ's resurrection, Mary had first to share in his death.

The New Testament provides no information on the circumstances of Mary's death. This silence leads one to suppose that it happened naturally, with no detail especially worthy of mention. If this were not the case, how could the information about it have remained hidden from her contemporaries and not have been passed down to us in some way?

As to the cause of Mary's death, the opinions seem groundless that wish to exclude her from death by natural causes. It is more important to look for the Blessed Virgin's spiritual attitude at the moment of her departure from this world. In this regard, St. Francis de Sales maintained that Mary's death was due to a transport of love. He speaks of a dying "in love for her Son Jesus" (*Treatise on the Love of God,* bk. 7, ch. 13–14).

Whatever from the physical point of view was the organic, biological cause of the end of her bodily life, it can be said that for Mary the passage from this life to the next was the full development of grace in glory, so that no death can ever be so fittingly described as a "dormition" as hers.

In some of the writings of the Church Fathers we find Jesus himself described as coming to take his Mother at the time of her death to bring her into heavenly glory. In this way they present the death of Mary as an event of love which conducted her to her divine Son to share his immortal life. At the end of her earthly life, she must have experienced, like Paul and more strongly, the desire to be freed from her body in order to be with Christ for ever (cf. Phil 1:23). The experience of death personally enriched the Blessed Virgin. By undergoing mankind's common destiny, she can more effectively exercise her spiritual motherhood toward those approaching the last moment of their lives.

General audience of June 25, 1997

The Church Believes
in Mary's Assumption

Following the Bull *Munificentissimus Deus* of my venerable Predecessor Pius XII, the Second Vatican Council affirmed that the immaculate Virgin "on the completion of her earthly sojourn was taken up body and soul into heavenly glory" (*LG* 59). The Council Fathers wished to stress that Mary, unlike Christians who die in God's grace, was taken up into the glory of heaven with her body. This age-old belief is expressed in a long iconogaphical tradition which shows Mary "entering" heaven with her body.

The dogma of the assumption affirms that Mary's body was glorified after her death. While for other human beings the resurrection of the body will take place at the end of the world, for Mary the glorification of her body was anticipated by a special privilege.

On November 1, 1950, in defining the dogma of the assumption, Pius XII avoided using the term "resurrection" and did not take a position on the question of the Blessed Virgin's death as a truth of faith. The Bull *Munificentissimus Deus* limits itself to affirming the elevation of Mary's body to heavenly glory, declaring this truth a "divinely revealed dogma."

How can we not see that the assumption of the Blessed Virgin has always been part of the faith of the Christian people who, by affirming Mary's entrance into heavenly glory, have meant to proclaim the glorification of her body? The first trace of belief in the Virgin's assumption can be found in the apocryphal accounts entitled *Transitus Mariae,* whose origin dates to the second and third centuries. These are popular and sometimes romanticized depictions, which in this case, however, pick up an intuition of faith on the part of God's people.

Later, there was a long period of growing reflection on Mary's destiny in the next world. This gradually led the faithful to believe in the glorious raising of the Mother of Jesus in body and soul, and to the institution in the East of the liturgical feasts of the Dormition and Assumption of Mary.

Belief in the glorious destiny of the body and soul of the Lord's Mother after her death spread very rapidly from East to West and has been widespread since the 14th century. In our century, on the eve of the definition of the dogma it was a truth almost universally accepted and professed by the Christian community in every corner of the world.

Therefore, in May 1946, with the Encyclical *Deiparae Virginis Mariae,* Pius XII called for a broad consultation, inquiring among the bishops and through them among the clergy and the People of God as to the possibility and opportuness of defining the bodily assumption of Mary as a dogma of faith. The result was extremely positive: only six answers out of 1,181 showed any reservations about the revealed character of this truth.

Citing this fact, the Bull *Munificentissimus Deus* states: "From the universal agreement of the Church's ordinary magisterium we have a certain and firm proof demonstrating that the Blessed Virgin Mary's bodily assumption into heaven...is a truth revealed by God and therefore should be firmly and faithfully believed by all the children of the Church" (*Munificentissimus Deus: AAS* 42 [1950], 757).

The definition of the dogma, in conformity with the universal faith of the People of God, definitively excludes every doubt and calls for the express assent of all Christians. After stressing the Church's actual belief in the assumption, the Bull recalls the scriptural basis for this truth. Although the New Testament does not explicitly affirm Mary's assumption, it offers a basis for it because it strongly emphasizes the Blessed Virgin's perfect union with Jesus' destiny. This union, which was manifested from the time of the Mother's participation in her Son's mission and especially in her association with his redemptive sacrifice, cannot fail to require a continuation after death. Perfectly united with the life and saving work of Jesus, Mary shares his heavenly destiny in body and soul.

The Bull *Munificentissimus Deus* cited above refers to the participation of the woman of the Protogospel in the struggle against the serpent, recognizing Mary as the New Eve, and presents the assumption as a consequence of Mary's union with Christ's saving work. In this regard it says: "Consequently, just as the glorious resurrection of Christ was an essential part and the final sign of this victory, so that struggle which was common to the Blessed Virgin and her divine Son should be brought to a close by the glorification of her virginal body" (*Munificentissimus Deus: AAS* 42 [1950], 768).

Therefore, the assumption is the culmination of the struggle which involved Mary's generous love in the redemption of humanity and is the fruit of her unique sharing in the victory of the cross.

General audience of July 2, 1997

Mary Is the First Creature to Enjoy Eternal Life

The Church's constant and unanimous tradition shows how Mary's assumption is part of the divine plan and is rooted in her unique sharing in the mission of her Son. In the first millennium sacred authors had already spoken in this way. Testimonies, not yet fully developed, can be found in St. Ambrose, St. Epiphanius and Timothy of Jerusalem. St. Germanus I of Constantinople (d. 730) puts these words on Jesus' lips as he prepares to take his Mother to heaven: "You must be where I am, Mother inseparable from your Son..." (*Hom. 3* in *Dormitionem, PG* 98, 360).

In addition, the same ecclesial tradition sees the fundamental reason for the assumption in the divine motherhood. We find an interesting trace of this conviction in a fifth-century apocryphal account attributed to Pseudo-Melito. The author imagines Christ questioning Peter and the apostles on the destiny Mary deserved and this is the reply he received: "Lord, you chose this handmaid of yours to become an immaculate dwelling place for you.... Thus it seemed right to us, your servants, that just as you reign in glory after conquering death, so you should raise your Mother's body and take her rejoicing with you to heaven" (*Transitus Mariae,* 16, *PG* 5, 1238). It can therefore be said that the divine motherhood, which made Mary's body the immaculate dwelling place of the Lord, was the basis of her glorious destiny.

St. Germanus maintains in a richly poetic text that Jesus' affection for his Mother requires Mary to be united with her divine Son in heaven: "Just as a child seeks and desires its mother's presence and a mother delights in her child's company, it was fitting that you, whose motherly love for your Son and God leaves no room for doubt, should return to him. And was it not right, in any case, that this God who had a truly filial love for you, should take you into his company?" (*Hom. 1 in Dormitionem, PG* 98, 347). In another text, the venerable author combines the private aspect of the relationship between Christ and Mary with the saving dimension of her motherhood, maintaining that "the Mother of Life should share the dwelling place of Life" (*Ibid., PG* 98, 348).

According to some of the Church Fathers, another argument for the privilege of the assumption is taken from Mary's sharing in the work of redemption. St. John Damascene underscores the relationship between her participation in the passion and her glorious destiny: "It was right that she who had seen her Son on the cross and received the sword of sorrow in the depths of her heart...should behold this Son seated at the right hand of the Father" (*Hom. 2, PG* 96, 741). In the light of the Paschal Mystery, it appears particularly clear that the Mother should also be glorified with her Son after death.

Recalling the mystery of the assumption in the *Dogmatic Constitution on the Church,* the Second Vatican Council drew attention to the privilege of the immaculate conception. Precisely because she was "preserved free from all guilt of original sin" (*LG* 59), Mary could not remain like other human beings in the state of death until the end of the world. The absence of original sin and her perfect holiness from the very first moment of her existence required the full glorification of the body and soul of the Mother of God.

Looking at the mystery of the Blessed Virgin's assumption, we can understand the plan of divine providence for humanity. After Christ, the incarnate Word, Mary is the first human being to achieve the eschatological ideal, anticipating the fullness of happiness promised to the elect through the resurrection of the body.

In the assumption of the Blessed Virgin we can also see the divine will to advance woman. In a way analogous to what happened at the beginning of the human race and of salvation history, in God's plan the eschatological ideal was not to be revealed in an individual, but in a couple. Thus, in heavenly glory, beside the risen Christ there is a woman who has been raised up, Mary: the New Adam and the New Eve, the first fruits of the general resurrection of the bodies of all humanity.

The eschatological conditions of Christ and Mary should not, of course, be put on the same level. Mary, the New Eve, received from Christ, the New Adam, the fullness of grace and heavenly glory, having been raised through the Holy Spirit by the sovereign power of the Son.

Despite their brevity, these notes enable us to show clearly that Mary's assumption reveals the nobility and dignity of the human body. In the face of the profanation and debasement to which modern society frequently subjects the female body, the mystery of the assumption proclaims the supernatural destiny and dignity of every human body, called by the Lord to become an instrument of holiness and to share in his glory.

Mary entered into glory because she welcomed the Son of God in her virginal womb and in her heart. By looking at her, the Christian learns to discover the value of his own body and to guard it as a temple of God, in expectation of the resurrection. The assumption, a privilege granted to the Mother of God, thus has immense value for the life and destiny of humanity.

General audience of July 9, 1997

Christians Look to Mary, Queen

Popular devotion invokes Mary as queen. After recalling the assumption of the Blessed Virgin in "body and soul into heavenly glory," the Council explained that she was "exalted by the Lord as queen of the universe, that she might be the more fully conformed to her Son, the Lord of lords (cf. Rv 19:16) and the conqueror of sin and death" (*LG* 59).

Starting from the fifth century, almost in the same period in which the Council of Ephesus proclaimed her "Mother of God," the title of queen begins to be attributed to her. With this further recognition of her sublime dignity, the Christian people want to place her above all creatures, exalting her role and importance in the life of every person and of the whole world.

Already a fragment of a homily, attributed to Origen, contains this comment on the words Elizabeth spoke at the visitation: "It is I who should have come to visit you, because you are blessed above all women; you are the Mother of my Lord; you are my Lady" (*Fragment, PG* 13, 1902 D). The text passes spontaneously from the expression "the Mother of my Lord" to the title, "my Lady," anticipating what St. John Damascene was later to say. He attributed to Mary the title of "Sovereign": "When she became Mother of the Creator, she truly became queen of all creatures" (*De Fide Orthodoxa,* 4, 14, *PG* 94, 1157).

In his Encyclical *Ad Coeli Reginam* to which the text of *Lumen Gentium* refers, my venerable Predecessor Pius XII indicates Mary's cooperation in the work of the redemption, in addition to her motherhood, as the basis for her queenship. The encyclical recalls the liturgical text: "There was St. Mary, Queen of Heaven and sovereign of the world, sorrowing near the cross of our Lord Jesus Christ" (*AAS* 46 [1954], 634). It then establishes an analogy between Mary and Christ, which helps us understand the significance of the Blessed Virgin's royal status. Christ is king not only because he is Son of God, but also because he is the Redeemer. Mary is queen not only because she is Mother of God, but also because, associated as the New Eve with the New Adam, she cooperated in the work of the redemption of the human race (*AAS* 46 [1954], 635).

In Mark's Gospel, we read that on the day of the ascension the Lord Jesus "was taken up into heaven, and sat down at the right hand of God" (16:19). In biblical language, "to sit at the right hand of God" means sharing his sovereign power. Sitting "at the right hand of the Father," he establishes his kingdom, God's kingdom. Taken up into heaven, Mary is associated with the power of her Son and is dedicated to the extension of the kingdom, sharing in the diffusion of divine grace in the world.

In looking at the analogy between Christ's ascension and Mary's assumption, we can conclude that Mary, in dependence on Christ, is the queen who possesses and exercise over the universe a sovereignty granted to her by her Son.

The title of queen does not of course replace that of Mother. Her queenship remains a corollary of her particular maternal mission and simply expresses the power conferred on her to carry out that mission. Citing Pius IX's Bull *Ineffabilis Deus,* the Supreme Pontiff highlights this maternal dimension of the Blessed Virgin's queenship: "Having a motherly affection for us and being concerned for our salvation, she extends her care to the whole human race. Appointed by the Lord as queen of heaven and earth, raised above all the choirs of angels and the whole celestial hierarchy of saints, sitting at the right hand of her only Son our Lord Jesus Christ, she obtains with great certainty what she asks with her motherly prayers; she obtains what she seeks and it cannot be denied her" (cf. *AAS* 46 [1954], 636–637).

Therefore, Christians look with trust to Mary Queen and this not only does not diminish but indeed exalts their filial abandonment to her, who is mother in the order of grace. Indeed, the concern Mary Queen has for mankind can be fully effective precisely by virtue of her glorious state which derives from the assumption. St. Germanus I of Constantinople highlights this very well. He holds that this state guarantees Mary's intimate relationship with her Son and enables her to intercede in our favor. Addressing Mary he says: Christ wanted "to have, so to speak, the closeness of your lips and your heart; thus, he assents to all the desires you express to him; when you suffer for your children, with his divine power he does all that you ask of him" (*Hom. 1, PG* 98, 348).

One can conclude that the assumption favors Mary's full communion not only with Christ, but with each one of us. She is beside us, because her glorious state enables her to follow us in our daily earthly journey. As we read again in St. Germanus: "You dwell spiritually with us and the greatness of your vigilance over us makes your communion of life with us stand out" (*Hom. 1, PG* 98, 344).

Thus, far from creating distance between her and us, Mary's glorious state brings about a continuous and caring closeness. She knows everything that happens in our life and supports us with maternal love in life's trials. Taken up into heavenly glory, Mary dedicates herself totally to the work of salvation in order to communicate to every living person the happiness granted to her. She is a queen who gives all that she possesses, participating above all in the life and love of Christ.

General audience of July 23, 1997

Mary Is a Preeminent
Member of the Church

Mary's exceptional role in the work of salvation invites us to deepen the relationship that exists between her and the Church. According to some people Mary cannot be considered a member of the Church, since the privileges conferred on her—the immaculate conception, her divine motherhood and her unique cooperation in the work of salvation—place her in a condition of superiority with respect to the community of believers.

The Second Vatican Council, however, did not hesitate to present Mary as a member of the Church, nevertheless specifying that she is "a preeminent and singular member of the Church" (*LG* 53). Mary is the type of the Church, and its model and mother. Differing from all the other faithful because of the exceptional gifts she received from the Lord, the Blessed Virgin nonetheless belongs to the Church and is fully entitled to be a member.

Conciliar teaching finds a significant basis in Sacred Scripture. The Book of Acts shows Mary present from the beginning of the primitive community (cf. Acts 1:14), while she shared with the disciples and some women believers the prayerful expectation of the Holy Spirit, who would descend on them.

After Pentecost, the Blessed Virgin continued to live in fraternal communion with the community and took part in the prayers, in listening to the apostles' teaching, and in the "breaking of bread," that is, in the Eucharistic celebration (cf. Acts 2:42). She who had lived in close union with Jesus in the house of Nazareth lived in the Church in intimate communion with her Son, present in the Eucharist.

Mother of the only-begotten Son of God, Mary is Mother of the community which constitutes Christ's Mystical Body, and she guided its first steps. In accepting this mission, she was committed to encouraging ecclesial life with her maternal and exemplary presence. This solidarity derived from her belonging to the community of the redeemed. Unlike her Son, she needed redemption. Since "she belongs to the offspring of Adam she is one with all those who are to be saved" (*LG* 53). The privilege of the immaculate conception preserved her from the stain of sin, because of the Redeemer's special saving influence.

As "a preeminent and singular member of the Church," Mary uses the gifts God has granted her to achieve fuller solidarity with the brothers and sisters of her Son, who are now her children too.

As a member of the Church, Mary places her personal holiness, the fruit of God's grace and of her faithful collaboration, at the service of her brothers and sisters. The immaculate Virgin is an unfailing support for all Christians in their fight against sin and a constant encouragement to live as children of the Father who are redeemed by Christ and sanctified by the Spirit.

As a member of the first community "Mary the Mother of Jesus," (Acts 1:14) was respected and venerated by all. Each one understood the preeminence of Mary who brought forth the Son of God, the one universal Savior. Furthermore, the virginal character of her motherhood allows her to witness to the extraordinary contribution to the Church's good offered by the one who, giving up human fruitfulness through docility to the Holy Spirit, put herself completely at the service of God's kingdom.

Called to collaborate intimately in her Son's sacrifice and the gift of the divine life to humanity, Mary continues her motherly work after Pentecost. The mystery of love contained in the cross inspires her apostolic zeal and commits her, as a member of the Church, to spreading the Good News.

The words of the crucified Christ on Golgotha: "Woman, behold your Son" (Jn 19:26), with which her role as the universal mother of believers is recognized, unfold before her motherhood with new and limitless horizons. The gift of the Holy Spirit, received at Pentecost through the exercise of this mission, induces her to offer the help of her motherly heart to all who are on their way toward the total fulfillment of God's kingdom.

A preeminent member of the Church, Mary lives a unique relationship with the divine persons of the most holy Trinity: with the Father, the Son and the Holy Spirit. In calling her "Mother of the Son of God" and therefore "beloved daughter of the Father and the temple of the Holy Spirit" (*LG* 53), the Council recalled the primary effect of the Father's love, which is the divine motherhood.

Aware of the gift she has received, Mary shares with believers the attitudes of filial obedience and heartfelt gratitude. She encourages each one to recognize the signs of divine benevolence in his own life.

The Council used the expression "temple" *(sacrarium)* of the Holy Spirit, intending to emphasize the link of presence, love and collaboration that exists between the Blessed Virgin and the Holy Spirit. The Blessed Virgin, who was already invoked by Francis of Assisi as the "Bride of the Holy Spirit"

(Antiphon "Santa Maria Vergine" in *Fonti Francescane,* 281), by her example encourages the other members of the Church to entrust themselves generously to the mysterious action of the Paraclete, and to live with him in a constant communion of love.

General audience of July 30, 1997

Mary Is an Outstanding Figure of the Church

After presenting Mary as "a preeminent and singular member of the Church," *Lumen Gentium* declares her to be the Church's "type and excellent exemplar in faith and charity" (*LG* 53). The Council Fathers attributed to Mary the function of "type," that is, figure of the Church, borrowing the term from St. Ambrose who expressed himself thus in his commentary on the annunciation: "Yes, she [Mary] is betrothed, but she is a virgin because she is a type of the Church which is immaculate but a bride; a virgin, she conceived us by the Spirit; a virgin, she gave birth to us without pain" (*In Ev. Sec. Luc.,* II, 7, *CCL* 14, 33, 102–106). Thus, Mary is a type of the Church because of her immaculate holiness, her virginity, her betrothal and her motherhood. St. Paul uses the word "type" to give tangible form to a spiritual reality. He sees in the crossing of the Red Sea by the People of Israel a "type" or image of Christian Baptism, and in the manna and in the water which gushed from the rock, a "type" or image of the Eucharistic food and drink (cf. 1 Cor 10:1–11).

By defining Mary as a type of the Church, the Council invites us to see in her the visible figure of the Church's spiritual reality and in her spotless motherhood, the announcement of the Church's virginal motherhood.

It is necessary to explain that, unlike the Old Testament images or types, which are only prefigurations of future realities, in Mary the spiritual reality signified is already eminently present. The Red Sea crossing described in the Book of Exodus is a saving event of liberation, but it was certainly not a baptism capable of remitting sins and giving new life. Likewise, the manna, a precious gift from Yahweh to his people wandering in the desert, contained nothing of the future reality of the Eucharist, the Body of the Lord, nor did the water which gushed from the rock already contain Christ's Blood, shed for the multitude.

The Exodus is the great work accomplished by Yahweh for his people, but it does not constitute the definitive spiritual redemption which Christ would achieve in the Paschal Mystery. Moreover, referring to Jewish practices, Paul recalls: "These are only a shadow of what is to come, but the substance belongs to Christ" (Col 2:17). This is echoed in the Letter to the Hebrews which, systematically developing this interpretation, presents the worship of the Old Covenant as "a copy and shadow of the heavenly sanctuary" (Heb 8:5).

In affirming that Mary is a type of the Church, however, the Council did not intend to equate her with the figures or types of the Old Testament, but instead to affirm that in her the spiritual reality proclaimed and represented is completely fulfilled. The Blessed Virgin is a type of the Church, not as an imperfect prefiguration, but as the spiritual fullness which will be found in various ways in the Church's life. The particular relationship that exists here between the image and the reality represented is based on the divine plan, which establishes a close bond between Mary and the Church. The plan of salvation which orders the prefigurations of the Old Testament to fulfillment in the New Covenant likewise determined that Mary would live in a perfect way what was later to be fulfilled in the Church. The perfection God conferred upon Mary, therefore, acquires its most authentic meaning if it is interpreted as a prelude to divine life in the Church.

After saying that Mary is a "type of the Church," the Council added that she is her "outstanding model" and example of perfection to be followed and imitated. Mary is an "outstanding model" because her perfection surpasses that of all the other members of the Church.

Significantly, the Council added that she carries out this role "in faith and in charity." Without forgetting that Christ is the first model, the Council suggested in this way that there are interior dispositions proper to the model realized in Mary, which help the Christian to establish an authentic relationship with Christ. By looking at Mary, the believer learns to live in deeper communion with Christ, to adhere to him with a living faith and to place his trust and his hope in him, loving him with his whole being.

The functions of "type and model of the Church" refer in particular to Mary's virginal motherhood and shed light on her particular place in the work of salvation. This basic structure of Mary's being is reflected in the motherhood and virginity of the Church.

General audience of August 6, 1997

Mary Is a Model for the Church's Motherhood

It is precisely in the divine motherhood that the Council perceived the basis of the special relationship between Mary and the Church. We read in *Lumen Gentium:* "By reason of the gift and role of divine maternity, by which she is united with her Son, the Redeemer, and with his singular graces and functions, the Blessed Virgin is also intimately united with the Church" (*LG* 63). *Lumen Gentium* constantly refers to this same presupposition to illustrate the prerogatives of "type" and "model" which the Blessed Virgin enjoys in relation to the Mystical Body of Christ: "In the mystery of the Church, which is itself rightly called mother and virgin, the Blessed Virgin stands out in eminent and singular fashion as exemplar both of virgin and mother" (*LG* 63).

Mary's motherhood is defined as "eminent and singular," since it represents a unique and unrepeatable fact: before carrying out her motherly role for humanity, Mary is the Mother of the only-begotten Son of God made man. On the other hand, the Church is a mother because she gives spiritual birth to Christ in the faithful, thus carrying out her maternal role for the members of the Mystical Body. In this way the Blessed Virgin is a superior model for the Church, precisely because of the uniqueness of her prerogative as Mother of God.

In reflecting on Mary's motherhood, *Lumen Gentium* recalls that it is also expressed in the eminent dispositions of her soul: "By her belief and obedience, not knowing man but overshadowed by the Holy Spirit, as the new Eve she brought forth on earth the very Son of the Father, showing an undefiled faith, not in the word of the ancient serpent, but in that of God's messenger" (*LG* 63). From these words it can be clearly seen that Mary's faith and obedience at the annunciation are virtues for the Church to imitate and, in a certain sense, they begin her motherly journey in service to men called to salvation.

The divine motherhood cannot be isolated from the universal dimension given to it in God's saving plan, which the Council did not hesitate to recognize: "The Son whom she brought forth is he whom God placed as the firstborn among many brethren (Rom 8:29), namely the faithful, in whose birth and education she cooperates with a maternal love" (*LG* 63).

The Church becomes a mother, taking Mary as her model. In this regard the Council says: "The Church indeed, contemplating her hidden sanctity, imitating her charity and faithfully fulfilling the Father's will, by receiving the Word of God in faith becomes herself a mother. By her preaching she brings forth to a new and immortal life the sons who are born to her in baptism, conceived of the Holy Spirit and born of God" (*LG* 64).

Analyzing this description of the Church's maternal work, we can note how the Christian's birth is linked here in a certain way to the birth of Jesus, as though a reflection of it. Christians are "conceived by the Holy Spirit," and therefore their birth, the fruit of preaching and Baptism, resembles the Savior's.

Moreover, in contemplating Mary, the Church imitates her charity, her faithful acceptance of the Word of God and her docility in fulfilling the Father's will. By following the Blessed Virgin's example, she achieves a fruitful spiritual motherhood.

But the Church's motherhood does not make Mary's superfluous. Continuing to exercise her influence on the life of Christians, Mary helps to give the Church a maternal face. In the light of Mary the motherhood of the ecclesial community, which might seem somewhat general, is called to be expressed in a more concrete and personal way toward every person redeemed by Christ. By showing herself to be the Mother of all believers, Mary fosters in them relations of authentic spiritual brotherhood and constant dialogue.

The daily experience of faith in every age and place highlights the need many feel to entrust their daily necessities to Mary. They trustfully open their hearts to implore her motherly intercession and obtain her reassuring protection. The prayers addressed to Mary by people in every age, the many forms and expressions of Marian devotion, and the pilgrimages to shrines and places which commemorate the miracles worked by God the Father through the Mother of his Son show Mary's extraordinary influence on the Church's life. The love of the People of God for the Blessed Virgin points to the need for close personal relations with their heavenly Mother. At the same time Mary's spiritual motherhood supports and increases the Church's concrete practice of her own motherhood.

The two mothers, the Church and Mary, are both essential to Christian life. It could be said that the one is a more objective motherhood and the other more interior. The Church becomes a mother in preaching God's Word and administering the sacraments, particularly Baptism, in celebrating the Eucharist and in forgiving sins.

Mary's motherhood is expressed in all areas where grace is distributed, especially within the framework of personal relations. They are two inseparable forms of motherhood; both enable us to recognize the same divine love which seeks to share itself with mankind.

General audience of August 13, 1997

Mary Fully Adhered to Revealed Truth

The Church is a mother and a virgin. After affirming that she is a mother, modeled on Mary, the Council gives the Church the title of virgin, explaining its significance: "She herself is a virgin, who keeps whole and entire the faith given to her by her spouse. Imitating the mother of her Lord, and by the power of the Holy Spirit, she keeps with virginal purity an entire faith, a firm hope and a sincere charity" (*LG* 64).

Thus, Mary is also a model of the Church's virginity. In this regard, it is necessary to explain that virginity does not belong to the Church in the strict sense, since it does not represent the state of life of the vast majority of the faithful. By virtue of God's providential plan, marriage is the most widespread and we could say common state for those called to the faith. The gift of virginity is reserved to a limited number of the faithful, who are called to a particular mission within the ecclesial community.

Nevertheless, in mentioning St. Augustine's teaching, the Council maintained that the Church is virginal in the spiritual sense of integrity in faith, hope and charity. Therefore, the Church is not a virgin in the body of all her members, but possesses a virginity of the spirit *(virginitas mentis),* that is, "integral faith, firm hope and sincere charity" (*Tract. in Ev. Ioannis,* 13, 12; *PL* 35, 1499).

Lumen Gentium, therefore, takes pains to recall that Mary's virginity, a model for that of the Church, also includes the physical dimension, by which she virginally conceived Jesus by the power of the Holy Spirit without man's intervention.

Mary is a virgin in body and a virgin in heart, as appears from her intention to live in deep intimacy with the Lord, decisively manifested at the time of the annunciation. Thus she who is invoked as "Virgin of virgins" is without doubt for everyone a lofty example of purity and of total self-giving to the Lord. But she is a special source of inspiration for Christian virgins and for those who are radically and exclusively dedicated to the Lord in the various forms of consecrated life. Thus, after its important role in the work of salvation, Mary's virginity continues to have a beneficial influence on the Church's life.

Let us not forget that Christ is certainly the first and highest example for every chaste life. However, Mary is a special model of chastity lived for love of the Lord Jesus. She encourages all Christians to live chastity with particular commitment according to their own state, and to entrust themselves to the Lord in the different circumstances of life. She who is the sanctuary of the Holy Spirit *par excellence* helps believers rediscover their own body as the temple of God (cf. 1 Cor 6:19) and to respect its nobility and holiness.

Young people seeking genuine love look to the Blessed Virgin and invoke her motherly help to persevere in purity. Mary reminds married couples of the fundamental values of marriage by helping them overcome the temptation to discouragement and to subdue the passions that try to sway their hearts. Her total dedication to God is a strong encouragement to them to live in mutual fidelity, so that they will never give in to the difficulties that beset conjugal communion. The Council urged the faithful to look to Mary so that they may imitate her "virginally integral" faith, hope and charity.

To preserve the integrity of the faith is a demanding task for the Church, which is called to constant vigilance even at the cost of sacrifice and struggle. The Church's faith is not only threatened by those who reject the Gospel message, but especially by those who, in accepting only part of the revealed truth, refuse to share fully in the entire patrimony of the faith of Christ's bride.

Unfortunately, this temptation, which we find from the Church's beginning, continues to be present in her life, urging her to accept revelation only in part, or to give the Word of God a limited, personal interpretation in conformity with the prevailing mentality and individual desires. Having fully adhered to the Word of the Lord, Mary represents for the Church an unsurpassable model of "virginally integral" faith, for with docility and perseverance she accepts the revealed truth whole and entire. By her constant intercession, she obtains for the Church the light of hope and the flame of charity. In her earthly life, Mary was an incomparable example of these virtues for everyone.

General audience of August 20, 1997

Mary Is a Model of
Faith, Hope and Charity

In the Letter to the Ephesians, St. Paul explains the spousal relationship between Christ and the Church in the following words: "Christ loved the Church and gave himself up for her, that he might sanctify her, having cleansed her by the washing of water with the word, that he might present the Church to himself in splendor, without spot or wrinkle or any such thing, that she might be holy and without blemish" (Eph 5:25–27).

The Second Vatican Council took up the Apostle's assertions and recalled that "while in the most holy Virgin the Church has already reached that perfection whereby she is without spot or wrinkle, the followers of Christ still strive to increase in holiness by conquering sin" (*LG* 65).

In this way the difference between Mary and the faithful is emphasized, although both belong to the holy Church which Christ made "without spot or wrinkle." While the faithful have been freed "from the law of sin" (cf. Rom 8:2), they can still give in to temptation, and human frailty continues to manifest itself in their lives. "We all make many mistakes," says the Letter of James (3:2). For this reason the Council of Trent teaches: "No one can avoid all sins, even venial sins, throughout his life" (*DS* 1573). By divine privilege, however, the immaculate Virgin is an exception to this rule, as the Council of Trent itself recalls (cf. *DS* 1573).

Despite the sins of her members, the Church is first and foremost the community of those who are called to holiness and strive each day to achieve it. In this arduous path to perfection they feel encouraged by Mary, who is the "model of virtues." The Council noted: "Piously meditating on her and contemplating her in the light of the Word made man, the Church with reverence enters more intimately into the great mystery of the Incarnation and becomes more and more like her spouse" (*LG* 65).

So the Church looks to Mary. The Church not only contemplates the wondrous gift of Mary's fullness of grace, but strives to imitate the perfection which in her is the fruit of her full compliance with Christ's command: "You, therefore, must be perfect as your heavenly Father is perfect" (Mt 5:48). Mary is all holy. For the community of believers she represents the paradigm of the authentic holiness that is achieved in union with Christ. The earthly life of the Mother of God was characterized by perfect harmony with the person of her Son and by her total dedication to the redeeming work he accomplished.

The Church turns her gaze to the maternal intimacy that grew in silence during life in Nazareth and reached perfection at the moment of sacrifice, and she strives to imitate it in her daily journey. In this way, she is increasingly conformed to her spouse. United like Mary with the Redeemer's cross, the Church, amid the difficulties, contradictions and persecutions that renew in her life the mystery of her Lord's passion, constantly seeks to be fully configured to him.

The Church lives by faith, seeing in Mary "who believed that there would be a fulfillment of what was spoken to her from the Lord" (Lk 1:45), the first and perfect expression of her faith. On this journey of trusting abandonment to the Lord, the

Virgin goes before the disciples, adhering to the divine word with an increasing intensity that embraces all the stages of her life and spreads to the mission of the Church.

Mary's example encourages the People of God to practice their faith and to study and develop its content, by keeping it in their heart and meditating on the events of salvation.

Mary also becomes a model of hope for the Church. In listening to the angel's message, the Virgin first directs her hope to the kingdom without end, which Jesus had been sent to establish.

She stands firm near the cross of her Son, waiting for the divine promise to be fulfilled. After Pentecost, the Mother of Jesus sustains the Church's hope despite the threat of persecution. She is thus the Mother of hope for the community of believers and for individual Christians. She encourages and guides her children as they await the kingdom, supporting them in their daily trials and throughout the events of history, however tragic.

Lastly, the Church sees the model of her charity in Mary. By looking at the situation of the first Christian community, we discover that the unanimity of their hearts, which was shown as they awaited Pentecost, is associated with the presence of the holy Virgin (cf. Acts 1:14). Precisely because of Mary's radiant charity, it is possible to maintain harmony and fraternal love at all times within the Church.

The Council expressly underscored Mary's exemplary role for the Church's apostolic mission, with the following observation: "The Church, in her apostolic work also, justly looks to her, who brought forth Christ, who was conceived of the Holy Spirit and born of the Virgin, that through the Church he may be born and may increase in the hearts of the faithful also. The Virgin in her own life lived an example of that maternal love, by which it behooves that all should be animated who cooperate in the apostolic mission of the Church for the regeneration of men" (*LG* 65).

After having cooperated in the work of salvation by her motherhood, her association with Christ's sacrifice and her motherly aid to the newborn Church, Mary continues to support the Christian community and all believers in their generous commitment to proclaiming the Gospel.

General audience of September 3, 1997

Mary Is a Model
of the Church at Prayer

In the Apostolic Exhortation *Marialis Cultus,* the Servant of God Paul VI, of venerable memory, presents the Blessed Virgin as a model of the Church at worship. This assertion is a corollary to the truth that points to Mary as a paradigm for the People of God on the way to holiness: "That the Blessed Virgin is an exemplar in this field derives from the fact that she is recognized as a most excellent exemplar of the Church in the order of faith, charity and perfect union with Christ, that is, of that interior disposition with which the Church, the beloved spouse, closely associated with her Lord, invokes Christ and through him worships the eternal Father" (*MC* 16).

She who at the annunciation showed total availability for the divine plan represents for all believers a sublime model of attentiveness and docility to the Word of God. In replying to the angel: "Let it be to me according to your word" (Lk 1:38), and in stating her readiness to fulfill perfectly the Lord's will, Mary rightly shares in the beatitude proclaimed by Jesus: "Blessed are those who hear the Word of God and keep it" (Lk 11:28).

With this attitude, which encompassed her entire life, the Blessed Virgin indicates the high road of listening to the Word of the Lord, an essential element of worship, which has become typical of the Christian liturgy. Her example shows us that worship does not primarily consist in expressing human thoughts and feelings, but in listening to the divine word in order to know it, assimilate it and put it into practice in daily life.

Every liturgical celebration is a memorial of the mystery of Christ in his salvific action for all humanity and is meant to promote the personal participation of the faithful in the Paschal Mystery, re-expressed and made present in the gestures and words of the rite.

Mary was a witness to the historical unfolding of the saving events, which culminated in the Redeemer's death and resurrection. Mary kept "all these things, pondering them in her heart" (Lk 2:19). She was not merely present at the individual events, but sought to grasp their deep meaning, adhering with all her soul to what was being mysteriously accomplished in them.

Mary appears, therefore, as the supreme model of personal participation in the divine mysteries. She guides the Church in meditating on the mystery celebrated and in participating in the saving event, by encouraging the faithful to desire an intimate, personal relationship with Christ in order to cooperate with the gift of their own lives in the salvation of all.

Mary also represents the model of the Church at prayer. In all probability Mary was absorbed in prayer when the angel Gabriel came to her house in Nazareth and greeted her. This prayerful setting certainly supported the Blessed Virgin in her reply to the angel and in her generous assent to the mystery of the Incarnation.

In the annunciation scene, artists have almost always depicted Mary in a prayerful attitude. Of them all we recall Fra Angelico. This shows to the Church and every believer the atmosphere that should prevail during worship. We could add that for the People of God, Mary represents the model of every expression of their prayer life. In particular, she teaches Christians how to turn to God to ask for his help and support in the various circumstances of life.

Her motherly intercession at the wedding in Cana and her presence in the upper room at the apostles' side as they prayed in expectation of Pentecost suggest that the prayer of petition is an essential form of cooperation in furthering the work of salvation in the world. By following her model, the Church learns to be bold in her asking, to persevere in her intercessions and, above all, to implore the gift of the Holy Spirit (cf. Lk 11:13).

The Blessed Virgin also represents the Church's model for generously participating in sacrifice.

In presenting Jesus in the Temple and especially at the foot of the cross, Mary completes the gift of herself which associates her as Mother with the suffering and trials of her Son. Thus, in daily life as in the Eucharistic celebration, the "Virgin presenting offerings" (*MC* 20) encourages Christians to "offer spiritual sacrifices acceptable to God through Jesus Christ" (1 Pt 2:5).

General audience of September 10, 1997

The Blessed Virgin
Is Mother of the Church

After proclaiming Mary a "preeminent member," the "type" and "model" of the Church, the Second Vatican Council said: "The Catholic Church, taught by the Holy Spirit, honors her with filial affection and piety as a most beloved mother" (*LG* 53). The conciliar text does not explicitly attribute the title "Mother of the Church" to the Blessed Virgin, but it unmistakably expresses its content by repeating a statement made in 1748, more than two centuries ago, by Pope Benedict XIV (*Bullarium Romanum,* series 2, t. 2, n. 61, p. 428). In this document my venerable Predecessor, in describing the filial sentiments of the Church, which recognizes Mary as her most beloved mother, indirectly proclaims her Mother of the Church.

This title was rather rarely used in the past, but has recently become more common in the pronouncements of the Church's Magisterium and in the devotion of the Christian people. The faithful first called upon Mary with the title "Mother of God," "Mother of the faithful" or "our Mother," to emphasize her personal relationship with each of her children. Later, because of the greater attention paid to the mystery of the Church and to Mary's relationship to her, the Blessed Virgin began more frequently to be invoked as Mother of the Church. Before the Second Vatican Council, this expression was found in Pope Leo XIII's magisterium, which affirmed that Mary is "in all

234 THEOTÓKOS WOMAN, MOTHER, DISCIPLE

truth Mother of the Church" (*Acta Leonis XIII,* 15, 302). The title was later used many times in the teachings of John XXIII and Paul VI.

Although the title "Mother of the Church" was only recently attributed to Mary, it expresses the Blessed Virgin's maternal relationship with the Church as shown already in several New Testament texts. Since the annunciation, Mary was called to give her consent to the coming of the messianic kingdom which would take place with the formation of the Church. When at Cana Mary asked her Son to exercise his messianic power, she made a fundamental contribution to implanting the faith in the first community of disciples. She cooperated in initiating God's kingdom, which has its "seed" and "beginning" in the Church (cf. *LG* 5).

On Calvary, Mary united herself to the sacrifice of her Son and made her own maternal contribution to the work of salvation, which took the form of labor pains, the birth of the new humanity. In addressing the words "Woman, behold your son" to Mary, the crucified one proclaimed her motherhood not only in relation to the Apostle John but also to every disciple. The evangelist himself, by saying that Jesus had to die "to gather into one the children of God who are scattered abroad" (Jn 11:52), indicates the Church's birth as the fruit of the redemptive sacrifice with which Mary is maternally associated.

The Evangelist St. Luke mentions the presence of Jesus' Mother in the first community of Jerusalem (Acts 1:14). In this way he stresses Mary's maternal role in the newborn Church, comparing it to her role in the Redeemer's birth. The maternal dimension thus becomes a fundamental element of Mary's relationship with the new people of the redeemed.

Following Sacred Scripture, patristic teaching recognizes Mary's motherhood in the work of Christ and therefore in that of the Church, although in terms which are not always explicit. According to St. Irenaeus, Mary "became a cause of salvation for the whole human race" (*Adv. Haer.*, 3, 22, 4; *PG* 7, 959), and the pure womb of the Virgin "regenerates men in God" (*Adv. Haer.*, 4, 33, 11; *PG* 7, 1080). This is reechoed by St. Ambrose, who says: "A virgin has begotten the salvation of the world; a virgin has given life to all things" (*Ep.* 63, 33; *PL* 16, 1198), and by other Fathers who call Mary "Mother of salvation" (Severian of Gabala, *Or. 6 in mundi creationem,* 10, *PG* 54, 4; Faustus of Riez, *Max. bibl. patrum,* VI, 620–621).

In the Middle Ages, St. Anselm addressed Mary in this way: "You are the mother of justification and of the justified, the mother of reconciliation and of the reconciled, the mother of salvation and of the saved" (*Or.,* 52, 8; *PL* 158, 957), while other authors attribute to her the titles "Mother of grace" and "Mother of life."

The title "Mother of the Church" thus reflects the deep conviction of the Christian faithful, who see in Mary not only the mother of the person of Christ, but also of the faithful. She who is recognized as mother of salvation, life and grace, mother of the saved and mother of the living, is rightly proclaimed Mother of the Church.

Pope Paul VI would have liked the Second Vatican Council to have proclaimed "Mary Mother of the Church, that is, of the whole People of God, of the faithful and their pastors." He did so himself in his speech at the end of the Council's third session (November 21, 1964), also asking that "henceforth the Blessed Virgin be honored and invoked with this title by all the Christian people" (*AAS* 1964, 37).

In this way, my venerable Predecessor explicitly enunciated the doctrine contained in chapter eight of *Lumen Gentium,* hoping that the title of Mary, Mother of the Church, would have an even more important place in the liturgy and piety of the Christian people.

General audience of September 17, 1997

Mary Has a Universal Spiritual Motherhood

Mary is mother of humanity in the order of grace. The Second Vatican Council highlights this role of Mary, linking it to her cooperation in Christ's redemption. "By that decree of divine providence which determined the Incarnation of the Word, the Blessed Virgin was on this earth the virgin Mother of the Redeemer, and above all others and in a singular way the generous associate and humble handmaid of the Lord" (*LG* 61).

With these statements, *Lumen Gentium* gives proper emphasis to the fact that the Blessed Virgin was intimately associated with Christ's redemptive work, becoming the Savior's "generous associate," "in a singular way." With the actions of any mother, from the most ordinary to the most demanding, Mary freely cooperated in the work of humanity's salvation in profound and constant harmony with her divine Son.

The Council also pointed out that Mary's cooperation was inspired by the Gospel virtues of obedience, faith, hope and charity and was accomplished under the influence of the Holy Spirit. It also recalls that the gift of her universal spiritual motherhood stems precisely from this cooperation. Associated with Christ in the work of redemption, which includes the spiritual regeneration of humanity, she became mother of those reborn to new life.

In saying that Mary is "a mother to us in the order of grace" (cf. *LG* 61), the Council stressed that her spiritual motherhood is not limited to the disciples alone, as though the words Jesus spoke on Calvary, "Woman, behold your son" (Jn 19:26), required a restrictive interpretation. With these words the crucified one established an intimate relationship between Mary and his beloved disciple, a typological figure of universal scope, intending to offer his Mother as Mother to all mankind.

On the other hand, the universal efficacy of the redeeming sacrifice and Mary's conscious cooperation with Christ's sacrificial offering does not allow any limitation of her motherly love. Mary's universal mission is exercised in the context of her unique relationship with the Church. With her concern for every Christian, and indeed for every human creature, Mary guides the faith of the Church toward an ever deeper acceptance of God's Word, sustains her hope, enlivens her charity and fraternal communion and encourages her apostolic dynamism.

During her earthly life, Mary showed her spiritual motherhood to the Church for a very short time. Nonetheless, the full value of her role appeared after the assumption and is destined to extend down the centuries to the end of the world. The Council expressly stated: "This maternity of Mary in the order of grace began with the consent which she gave in faith at the annunciation and which she sustained without wavering beneath the cross, and lasts until the eternal fulfillment of all the elect" (*LG* 62). Having entered the Father's eternal kingdom, closer to her divine Son and thus closer to us all, she can more effectively exercise in the Spirit the role of maternal intercession entrusted to her by divine providence.

The heavenly Father wanted to place Mary close to Christ and in communion with him who can "save those who draw near to God through him, since he always lives to make intercession for them" (Heb 7:25). He wanted to unite to the Redeemer's intercession as a priest that of the Blessed Virgin as a mother. It is a role she carries out for the sake of those who are in danger and who need temporal favors and especially eternal salvation: "By her maternal charity, she cares for the brethren of her Son, who still journey on earth surrounded by dangers and difficulties, until they are led into the happiness of their true home. Therefore the Blessed Virgin is invoked by the Church under the titles of Advocate, Auxiliatrix, Adjutrix and Mediatrix" (*LG* 62).

The title "Advocate" goes back to St. Irenaeus. With regard to Eve's disobedience and Mary's obedience, he says that at the moment of the annunciation "the Virgin Mary became the Advocate" of Eve (*Adv. Haer.,* 5, 19, 1; *PG* 7, 1175–1176). With her "yes" she defended our first mother and freed her from the consequences of her disobedience, becoming the cause of salvation for her and the whole human race.

Mary exercises her role as "Advocate" by cooperating both with the Spirit (the Paraclete) and with the one who interceded on the cross for his persecutors (cf. Lk 23:34), whom John calls our "advocate with the Father" (1 Jn 2:1). As a mother, Mary defends her children and protects them from the harm caused by their own sins.

Christians call upon Mary as "Helper," recognizing her motherly love which sees her children's needs and is ready to come to their aid, especially when their eternal salvation is at stake. The conviction that Mary is close to those who are suffering or in situations of serious danger has prompted the faithful to invoke her as "Benefactress." The same trusting certainty is expressed in the most ancient Marian prayer with the words: "We fly to thy patronage, O holy Mother of God; despise not our petitions in our necessities but deliver us always from all dangers, O glorious and blessed Virgin" (from the *Liturgy of the Hours*). As maternal Mediatrix, Mary presents our desires and petitions to Christ, and transmits the divine gifts to us, interceding continually on our behalf.

General audience of September 24, 1997

Mary's Mediation Derives from Christ's

Among the titles attributed to Mary in the Church's devotion, chapter eight of *Lumen Gentium* recalls that of "Mediatrix." Although some Council Fathers did not fully agree with this choice of title (cf. *Acta Synodalia* III, 8, 163–164), it was nevertheless inserted into the *Dogmatic Constitution on the Church* as confirmation of the value of the truth it expresses. Care was therefore taken not to associate it with any particular theology of mediation, but merely to list it among Mary's other recognized titles. Moreover, the conciliar text had already described the meaning of the title "Mediatrix" when it said that Mary "by her constant intercession continues to bring us the gifts of eternal salvation" (*LG* 62).

As I recalled in my Encyclical *Redemptoris Mater:* "Mary's mediation is intimately linked with her motherhood. It possesses a specifically maternal character, which distinguishes it from the mediation of other creatures" (n. 38). From this point of view it is unique in its kind and singularly effective.

With regard to the objections made by some of the Council Fathers concerning the term "Mediatrix," the Council itself provided an answer by saying that Mary is "our Mother in the order of grace" (*LG* 61). We recall that Mary's mediation is essentially defined by her divine motherhood. Recognition of her role as mediatrix is moreover implicit in the expression "our Mother," which presents the doctrine of Marian mediation by putting the accent on her motherhood. Lastly, the title "Mother in the order of grace" explains that the Blessed Virgin cooperates with Christ in humanity's spiritual rebirth.

Mary's maternal mediation does not obscure the unique and perfect mediation of Christ. After calling Mary "mediatrix," the Council was careful to explain that this "neither takes away from nor adds anything to the dignity and efficaciousness of Christ the one Mediator" (*LG* 62). On this subject it quotes the famous text from the First Letter to Timothy: "For there is one God and there is one mediator between God and men, the man Christ Jesus, who gave himself as a ransom for all" (2:5–6). In addition, the Council stated: "The maternal duty of Mary toward men in no wise obscures or diminishes this unique mediation of Christ, but rather shows his power" (*LG* 60).

Therefore, far from being an obstacle to the exercise of Christ's unique mediation, Mary instead highlights its fruitfulness and efficacy. "The salvific influence of the Blessed Virgin on men originates, not from some inner necessity, but from the divine pleasure. It flows forth from the superabundance of the merits of Christ, rests on his mediation, depends entirely on it and draws all its power from it" (*LG* 60).

The value of Mary's mediation derives from Christ, and thus the salutary influence of the Blessed Virgin does not "impede, but rather does it foster the immediate union of the faithful with Christ" (*LG* 60).

The intrinsic orientation to Christ of the work of the Mediatrix spurred the Council to recommend that the faithful turn to Mary "so that, encouraged by this maternal help they may the more closely adhere to the Mediator and Redeemer" *(LG* 62). In proclaiming Christ the one mediator (cf. 1 Tm 2:5–6), the text of St. Paul's Letter to Timothy excludes any other parallel mediation, but not subordinate mediation. In fact, before emphasizing the one exclusive mediation of Christ, the author urges "that supplications, prayers, intercessions and thanksgivings be made for all men" (2:1). Are not prayers a form of mediation? Indeed, according to St. Paul, the unique mediation of Christ is meant to encourage other dependent, ministerial forms of mediation. By proclaiming the uniqueness of Christ's mediation, the Apostle intends only to exclude any autonomous or rival mediation and not other forms compatible with the infinite value of the Savior's work.

It is possible to participate in Christ's mediation in various areas of the work of salvation. After stressing that "no creature could ever be counted as equal with the incarnate Word and Redeemer" (n. 62), *Lumen Gentium* describes how it is possible for creatures to exercise certain forms of mediation which depend on Christ. "Just as the priesthood of Christ is shared in various ways both by the ministers and by the faithful, and as the one goodness of God is really communicated in different ways to his creatures, so also the unique mediation of the Redeemer does not exclude but rather gives rise to a manifold cooperation which is but a sharing in this one source" *(LG* 62). This desire to bring about various participations in the one mediation of Christ reveals the gratuitous love of God who wants to share what he possesses.

In truth, what is Mary's maternal mediation if not the Father's gift to humanity? This is why the Council concludes: "The Church does not hesitate to profess this subordinate role of Mary. It knows it through unfailing experience of it and commends it to the hearts of the faithful" *(LG* 62). Mary carries out her maternal role in constant dependence on the mediation of Christ, and from him receives all that his heart wishes to give mankind.

On her earthly pilgrimage the Church continuously experiences the effective action of her "Mother in the order of grace."

General audience of October 1, 1997

Mary Has Always Been Specially Venerated

"When the time had fully come, God sent forth his Son, born of woman" (Gal 4:4). Marian devotion is based on the wondrous divine decision, as the Apostle Paul recalls, to link forever the Son of God's human identity with a woman, Mary of Nazareth. The mystery of the divine motherhood and of Mary's cooperation in the work of redemption has filled believers in every age with an attitude of praise, both for the Savior and for Mary who gave birth to him in time, thus cooperating in redemption.

A further reason for grateful love for the Blessed Virgin is offered by her universal motherhood. By choosing her as Mother of all humanity, the heavenly Father has wished to reveal the motherly dimension, so to speak, of his divine tenderness and concern for all people in every era.

On Calvary, with the words: "Behold, your son!" "Behold your mother!" (Jn 19:26–27), Jesus gave Mary in advance to all who would receive the Good News of salvation, and was thus laying the foundation of their filial affection for her. Following John, the faithful would prolong Christ's love for his Mother with their own devotion, by accepting her into their own lives.

The Gospel texts attest to the presence of Marian devotion from the Church's origins. The first two chapters of St. Luke's

Gospel seem to relate the particular attention to Jesus' Mother on the part of Jewish Christians, who expressed their appreciation of her and jealously guarded their memories of her. Moreover, in the infancy narratives we can discern the initial expressions of and reasons for Marian devotion, summarized in Elizabeth's exclamations: "Blessed are you among women.... And blessed is she who believed that there would be a fulfillment of what was spoken to her from the Lord" (Lk 1:42, 45).

Traces of a veneration already widespread among the first Christian community are present in the *Magnificat* canticle: "All generations will call me blessed" (Lk 1:48). By putting these words on Mary's lips, Christians recognized her unique greatness, which would be proclaimed until the end of time.

In addition, the Gospel accounts (cf. Lk 1:24–35; Mt 1:23; Jn 1:13), the first formulas of faith and a passage by St. Ignatius of Antioch (cf. *Smyrn.,* 1, 2: *SC* 10, 155) attest to the first communities' special admiration for Mary's virginity, closely linked to the mystery of the Incarnation. By noting Mary's presence at the beginning and at the end of her Son's public life, John's Gospel suggests that the first Christians were keenly aware of Mary's role in the work of redemption, in full loving dependence on Christ.

In stressing the particular character of Marian devotion, the Second Vatican Council said: "Placed by the grace of God, as God's Mother, next to her Son and exalted above all angels and men, Mary intervened in the mysteries of Christ and is justly honored by a special cult in the Church" (*LG* 66).

Then, alluding to the third-century Marian prayer, *Sub tuum praesidium*—"We fly to your protection"—it adds that this characteristic emerged from the very beginning: "From earliest times the Blessed Virgin is honored under the title of Mother of God, under whose protection the faithful took refuge in all their dangers and necessities" (*LG* 66).

This assertion has been confirmed in iconography and in the teaching of the Fathers of the Church since the second century. In Rome, in the catacombs of Priscilla, it is possible to admire the first depiction of the Madonna and child. At the same time, St. Justin and St. Irenaeus spoke of Mary as the new Eve who by her faith and obedience made amends for the disbelief and disobedience of the first woman. According to the Bishop of Lyons, it was not enough for Adam to be redeemed in Christ, but "it was right and necessary that Eve be restored in Mary" (*Demonstratio Apostolica,* 33). In this way he stressed the importance of woman in the work of salvation and laid the foundation for the inseparability of Marian devotion from that shown to Jesus, which would endure down the Christian centuries.

Marian devotion was first expressed in the invocation of Mary as *Theotókos,* a title which the Council of Ephesus authoritatively confirmed in 431, after the Nestorian crisis. The same popular reaction to the ambiguous and wavering position of Nestorius, who went so far as to deny Mary's divine motherhood, and the subsequent joyful acceptance of the Ephesian Synod's decisions, confirm how deeply rooted among Christians was devotion to the Blessed Virgin. However "after the Synod of Ephesus the cult of the People of God toward Mary wonderfully increased in veneration and love, in invocation and imitation" (*LG* 6). It was expressed especially in the liturgical feasts, among which, from the beginning of the fifth century, "the day of Mary *Theotókos*" acquired particular importance. It was celebrated on August 15th in Jerusalem and later became the feast of the Dormition or the Assumption. Under the influence of the *Proto-Evangelium of James,* the feasts of the Nativity, the Conception and the Presentation were also introduced, and notably contributed to highlighting some important aspects of the mystery of Mary.

We can certainly say that Marian devotion has developed down to our day in wonderful continuity, alternating between flourishing periods and critical ones that, nonetheless, often had the merit of fostering its renewal even more. Since the Second Vatican Council, Marian devotion seems destined to develop in harmony with a deeper understanding of the mystery of the Church and in dialogue with contemporary cultures, to be ever more firmly rooted in the faith and life of God's pilgrim people on earth.

General audience of October 15, 1997

Devotion to Mary

The Second Vatican Council stated that devotion to the Blessed Virgin, "as it always existed, although it is altogether singular, differs essentially from the cult of adoration which is offered to the incarnate Word, as well to the Father and the Holy Spirit, and it is most favorable to it" (*LG* 66). With these words *Lumen Gentium* stresses the characteristics of Marian devotion. Although the veneration of the faithful for Mary is superior to their devotion to the other saints, it is nevertheless inferior to the cult of adoration reserved to God, from which it essentially differs. The term "adoration" indicates the form of worship that man offers to God, acknowledging him as Creator and Lord of the universe. Enlightened by divine revelation, the Christian adores the Father "in spirit and truth" (Jn 4:23). With the Father, he adores Christ, the incarnate Word, exclaiming with the Apostle Thomas: "My Lord and my God!" (Jn 20:28). Lastly, in this same act of adoration he includes the Holy Spirit, who "with the Father and the Son is worshiped and glorified" (*DS* 150), as the Nicene-Constantinopolitan Creed recalls.

When the faithful call upon Mary as "Mother of God" and contemplate in her the highest dignity conferred upon a creature, they are still not offering her a veneration equal to that of the divine Persons. There is an infinite distance between

Marian veneration and worship of the Trinity and the incarnate Word.

As a consequence, although the Christian community addresses the Blessed Virgin in language that sometimes recalls the terms used in the worship of God, it has a completely different meaning and value. Thus, the love of the faithful for Mary differs from what they owe God. While the Lord must be loved above everything with all one's heart, with all one's soul and with all one's mind (cf. Mt 22:37), the sentiment joining Christians to the Blessed Virgin suggests, at a spiritual level, the affection of children for their mother.

Nevertheless, there is a continuity between Marian devotion and the worship given to God. The honor paid to Mary is ordered and leads to adoration of the Blessed Trinity. The Council recalled that Christian veneration of the Blessed Virgin "is most favorable to" the worship of the incarnate Word, the Father and the Holy Spirit. It then added from a Christological viewpoint that "the various forms of piety toward the Mother of God, which the Church, within the limits of sound and orthodox doctrine, according to the conditions of time and place and the nature and ingenuity of the faithful has approved, bring it about that while the Mother is honored, the Son, through whom all things have their being (cf. Col 1:15–16) and in whom it has pleased the Father that all fullness should dwell (Col 1:19), is rightly known, loved and glorified, and that all his commands are observed" (*LG* 66).

Since the Church's earliest days, Marian devotion has been meant to foster faithful adherence to Christ. To venerate the Mother of God is to affirm the divinity of Christ. In proclaiming Mary *Theotókos,* "Mother of God," the Fathers of the Council of Ephesus intended to confirm belief in Christ, true God.

The conclusion of the account of Jesus' first miracle, obtained at Cana by Mary's intercession, shows how her action was directed to the glorification of her Son. The evangelist says: "This, the first of his signs, Jesus did at Cana in Galilee and manifested his glory, and his disciples believed in him" (Jn 2:11).

Marian devotion also encourages adoration of the Father and the Holy Spirit in those who practice it according to the Church's spirit. By recognizing the value of Mary's motherhood, believers discover in it a special manifestation of God the Father's tenderness. The mystery of the virgin Mother highlights the action of the Holy Spirit, who brought about the conception of the child in her womb and continually guided her life. The titles of Comforter, Advocate, Helper—attributed to Mary by popular Christian piety—do not overshadow but exalt the action of the Spirit, the Comforter and dispose believers to benefit from his gifts.

Lastly, the Council recalled the "uniqueness" of Marian devotion and stressed the difference between adoration of God and veneration of the saints. This devotion is unrepeatable because it is directed to a person whose personal perfection and mission are unique. The gifts conferred upon Mary by divine love, such as her immaculate holiness, her divine motherhood, her association with the work of redemption and above all the sacrifice of the cross, are absolutely exceptional.

Devotion to Mary expresses the Church's praise and recognition of these extraordinary gifts. To Mary, who is Mother of the Church and Mother of humanity, the Christian people turn, encouraged by filial trust, to request her motherly intercession and to obtain the necessary goods for earthly life in view of eternal happiness.

General audience of October 22, 1997

The Church Urges
the Faithful to Venerate Mary

After giving doctrinal justification to veneration of the Blessed Virgin, the Second Vatican Council exhorted all the faithful to promote it: "This most holy synod deliberately teaches this Catholic doctrine and at the same time admonishes all the sons of the Church that the cult, especially the liturgical cult, of the Blessed Virgin be generously fostered, and the practices and exercises of piety, recommended by the Magisterium of the Church toward her in the course of centuries, be made of great moment" (*LG* 67).

With this last statement the Council Fathers, without going into particulars, intended to reaffirm the validity of certain prayers such as the rosary and the Angelus. These are dear to the tradition of the Christian people and are frequently encouraged by the Supreme Pontiffs as an effective means of nourishing the life of faith and devotion to the Blessed Virgin.

The conciliar text goes on to ask believers that "those decrees, which have been given in the early days regarding the cult of images of Christ, the Blessed Virgin and the saints, be religiously observed" (*LG* 67). Thus, it reproposed the decisions of the Second Council of Nicea, held in 787, which confirmed the legitimacy of the veneration of sacred images in opposition to those who wished to destroy them, since they considered them inadequate for representing the divinity (cf. *RM* 33).

"We define," said the Fathers of that Council, "with full precision and care that, like the representation of the precious life-giving cross, so the venerated and holy images either painted or mosaic or made of any other suitable material, should be exposed in holy churches of God on sacred furnishings and vestments, on walls and panels in homes and streets, be they images of the Lord God and our Savior Jesus Christ, or of our immaculate Lady, the holy Mother of God, of the holy angels, or of all the saints and the just" (*DS* 600). By recalling this definition, *Lumen Gentium* intended to stress the legitimacy and validity of sacred images, in contrast to certain tendencies to remove them from churches and shrines in order to focus full attention on Christ.

The Second Council of Nicea not only affirmed the legitimacy of images, but sought to describe their usefulness for Christian piety: "Indeed, the more often these images are contemplated, the more those who look at them are brought to remember and desire the original models and, in kissing them, to show them respect and veneration" (*DS* 601). These directives apply in a particular way to the veneration of the Blessed Virgin. Images, icons and statues of our Lady, present in houses, public places and countless churches and chapels, help the faithful to invoke her constant presence and her merciful patronage in the various circumstances of life. By making the Blessed Virgin's motherly tenderness concrete and almost visible, they invite us to turn to her, to pray to her trustfully and to imitate her in generously accepting the divine will.

None of the known images is an authentic reproduction of Mary's face, as St. Augustine had already acknowledged (*De Trinitate,* 8, 7). However, they help us establish a more living relationship with her. Therefore, the practice of exposing images of Mary in places of worship and in other buildings should be encouraged, in order to be aware of her help in moments of difficulty and as a reminder to lead a life that is ever more holy and faithful to God.

To encourage the proper use of sacred images, the Council of Nicea recalled that "the honor paid to the image is really paid to the person it represents, and those who venerate the image are venerating the reality of the person it represents" (*DS* 601). Hence, in adoring the person of the incarnate Word in the image of Christ, the faithful are making a genuine act of worship, which has nothing in common with idolatry. Similarly, in venerating images of Mary, the believer's act is ultimately intended as a tribute to the person of the Mother of Jesus.

Therefore, the Second Vatican Council urged theologians and preachers to refrain from both exaggerating and minimizing the special dignity of the Mother of God. It added: "Following the study of Sacred Scripture, the holy Fathers, the doctors and liturgy of the Church, and under the guidance of the Church's Magisterium, let them rightly illustrate the duties and privileges of the Blessed Virgin which always look to Christ, the source of all truth, sanctity and piety" (*LG* 67).

Authentic Marian doctrine is ensured by fidelity to Scripture and Tradition, as well as to the liturgical texts and the magisterium. Its indispensable characteristic is the reference to Christ: everything in Mary derives from Christ and is directed to him.

Lastly, the Council offered believers several criteria for authentically living their filial relationship with Mary: "Let the faithful remember moreover that true devotion consists neither in sterile or transitory affection, nor in a certain vain credulity, but proceeds from true faith, by which we are led to know the excellence of the Mother of God, and we are moved to a filial love toward our mother and to the imitation of her virtues" (*LG* 67).

With these words, the Council Fathers put people on guard

against "vain credulity" and the predominance of sentiment. They aim above all at reaffirming authentic Marian devotion, which proceeds from faith and the loving recognition of Mary's dignity, fosters filial affection for her and inspires the firm resolution to imitate her virtues.

General audience of October 29, 1997

We Can Count on Mary's Intercession

Down the centuries Marian devotion has enjoyed an uninterrupted development. In addition to the traditional liturgical feasts dedicated to the Lord's Mother, there has been a flowering of countless expressions of piety, often approved and encouraged by the Church's Magisterium. Many Marian devotions and prayers are an extension of the liturgy itself and have sometimes contributed to its overall enrichment, as is the case with the Office in honor of the Blessed Virgin and other pious compositions which have become part of the breviary.

The first known Marian invocation goes back to the third century and begins with the words: "We fly to thy protection *(Sub tuum praesidium),* O holy Mother of God...." However, since the 14th century the most common prayer among Christians has been the Hail Mary.

By repeating the first words the angel addressed to Mary, it leads the faithful to contemplate the mystery of the Incarnation. The Latin word "ave" translates the Greek word *chaïré:* it is an invitation to joy and could be translated "rejoice." The Eastern hymn *Akathistos* repeatedly stresses this "rejoice." In the Hail Mary the Blessed Virgin is called "full of grace" and is thus recognized for the perfection and beauty of her soul.

The phrase "the Lord is with you" reveals God's special personal relationship with Mary, which fits into the great plan for his covenant with all humanity. Next, the statement "Blessed are you among women and blessed is the fruit of your womb, Jesus" expresses the fulfillment of the divine plan in the Daughter of Zion's virginal body. Calling upon "Holy Mary, Mother of God," Christians ask the one who was the immaculate mother of the Lord by a unique privilege to "pray for us sinners," and they entrust themselves to her at the present moment and at the ultimate moment of death.

The traditional prayer of the Angelus also invites Christians to meditate on the mystery of the Incarnation. It urges them to take Mary as their point of reference at different times of their day in order to imitate her willingness to fulfill the divine plan of salvation. This prayer makes us relive in a way that great event in human history, the Incarnation, to which every Hail Mary refers. Here we find the value and attraction of the Angelus, expressed so many times not only by theologians and pastors but also by poets and painters.

In Marian devotion the rosary has taken on an important role. By repeating the Hail Mary, it leads us to contemplate the mysteries of faith. In nourishing the Christian people's love for the Mother of God, this simple prayer also orients Marian prayer in a clearer way to its goal: the glorification of Christ.

Like his predecessors, especially Leo XIII, Pius XII and John XXIII, Pope Paul VI held the recitation of the rosary in great esteem and wished it to be widely spread among families. Moreover, in the Apostolic Exhortation *Marialis Cultus,* he explained its doctrine by recalling that it is a "Gospel prayer, centered on the mystery of the redemptive Incarnation," and stressed its "clearly Christological orientation" (n. 46).

Popular piety frequently adds a litany to the rosary. The best known is the one used at the shrine of Loreto and is therefore called the Litany of Loreto. With very simple invocations it helps us concentrate on Mary's person, in order to grasp the spiritual riches which the Father's love poured out in her.

As the liturgy and Christian piety demonstrate, the Church has always held devotion to Mary in high esteem, considering it inseparably linked to belief in Christ. It is based on the Father's plan, the Savior's will and the Paraclete's inspiration.

Having received salvation and grace from Christ, the Blessed Virgin is called to play an important role in humanity's redemption. Through Marian devotion Christians acknowledge the value of Mary's presence on their journey to salvation, having recourse to her for every kind of grace. They especially know that they can count on her motherly intercession to receive from the Lord everything necessary for growing in the divine life and for attaining eternal salvation.

As the many titles attributed to the Blessed Virgin and the continual pilgrimages to Marian shrines attest, the trust of the faithful in Jesus' Mother spurs them to call upon her for their daily needs. They are certain that her maternal heart cannot remain indifferent to the material and spiritual distress of her children. By encouraging the confidence and spontaneity of the faithful, devotion to the Mother of God thus helps to brighten their spiritual life and enables them to make progress on the demanding path of the beatitudes.

Lastly, we would like to recall that devotion to Mary, by highlighting the human dimension of the Incarnation, helps us better to discern the face of a God who shares the joys and sufferings of humanity, the "God-with-us" whom she conceived as man in her most pure womb, gave birth to, cared for and followed with unspeakable love from his days in Nazareth and Bethlehem to those of the cross and resurrection.

General audience of November 5, 1997

Our Separated Brethren Also Honor Mary

After explaining the relationship between Mary and the Church, the Second Vatican Council rejoiced in observing that the Blessed Virgin is also honored by Christians who do not belong to the Catholic community: "It gives great joy and comfort to this holy and general synod that even among the separated brethren there are some who give due honor to the Mother of our Lord and Savior..." (*LG* 69; cf. *RM* 29–34). In view of this fact, we can say that Mary's universal motherhood, even if it makes the divisions among Christians seem all the sadder, represents a great sign of hope for the ecumenical journey.

Because of a particular conception of grace and ecclesiology, many Protestant communities are opposed to Marian doctrine and devotion, maintaining that Mary's cooperation in the work of salvation prejudices Christ's unique mediation. In this view, devotion to Mary would compete in a way with the honor owed the Son.

In recent years, however, further study of the thought of the first Reformers has shed light on positions more open to Catholic doctrine. Luther's writings, for example, show love and veneration for Mary, extolled as a model of every virtue. He upheld the sublime holiness of the Mother of God and at times affirmed the privilege of the immaculate conception, sharing with other Reformers belief in Mary's perpetual virginity.

The study of Luther and Calvin's thought, as well as the analysis of some texts of evangelical Christians, have contributed to a renewed attention by some Protestants and Anglicans to various themes of Mariological doctrine. Some have even arrived at positions very close to those of Catholics regarding the fundamental points of Marian doctrine, such as her divine motherhood, virginity, holiness and spiritual motherhood.

The concern for stressing the presence of women in the Church encourages the effort to recognize Mary's role in salvation history. All these facts are so many reasons to have hope for the ecumenical journey. Catholics have a deep desire to be able to share with all their brothers and sisters in Christ the joy that comes from Mary's presence in life according to the Spirit.

Among the brethren who "give due honor to the Mother of our Lord and Savior," the Council mentions Eastern Christians, "who with devout mind and fervent impulse give honor to the Mother of God, ever-virgin" (*LG* 69). As we can see from their many expressions of devotion, veneration for Mary represents a significant element of communion between Catholics and Orthodox.

However, there remain some disagreements regarding the dogmas of the immaculate conception and the assumption, even if these truths were first expounded by certain Eastern theologians—one need only recall great writers like Gregory Palamas (d.1359), Nicholas Cabasilas (d. after 1369) and George Scholarios (d. after 1472).

These disagreements, however, are perhaps more a question of formulation than of content and must never make us forget our common belief in Mary's divine motherhood, her perpetual virginity, her perfect holiness and her maternal intercession with her Son. As the Second Vatican Council recalled, this "fervent impulse" and "devout mind" unite Catholics and Orthodox in devotion to the Mother of God.

At the end of *Lumen Gentium* the Council invites us to entrust the unity of Christians to Mary: "The entire body of the faithful pours forth urgent supplications to the Mother of God and Mother of men, that she, who aided the beginnings of the Church by her prayers, may now, exalted as she is above all the angels and saints, intercede before her Son in the fellowship of all the saints" (*LG* 69).

Just as Mary's presence in the early community fostered oneness of heart, which prayer strengthened and made visible (cf. Acts 1:14), so the most intense communion with her whom St. Augustine called the "Mother of unity" (*Sermo 192,* 2; *PL* 38, 1013) will be able to bring Christians to the point of enjoying the long-awaited gift of ecumenical unity.

We ceaselessly pray to the Blessed Virgin so that, just as at the beginning she supported the journey of the Christian community's oneness in prayer and the proclamation of the Gospel, so today she may obtain through her intercession reconciliation and full communion among all believers in Christ.

Mother of men, Mary knows well the needs and aspirations of humanity. The Council particularly asked her to intercede so that "all families of people, whether they are honored with the title of Christian or whether they still do not know the Savior, may be happily gathered together in peace and harmony into one People of God, for the glory of the most holy and undivided Trinity" (*LG* 69).

The peace, harmony and unity which the Church and humanity hope for still seem far away. Nevertheless, they are a gift of the Spirit to be constantly sought, as we learn from Mary and trust in her intercession. With this petition Christians share the expectation of Mary who, filled with the virtue of hope, sustains the Church on her journey to the future with God.

Having personally achieved happiness because she "believed that there would be a fulfillment of what was spoken to her from the Lord" (Lk 1:45), the Blessed Virgin accompanies believers—and the whole Church—so that in the world, amid the joys and sufferings of this life, they may be true prophets of the hope that never disappoints.

General audience of November 12, 1997

Index

BOOKS & MEDIA

The Daughters of St. Paul operate book and media centers at the following addresses. Visit, call or write the one nearest you today, or find us on the World Wide Web, www.pauline.org

CALIFORNIA
3908 Sepulveda Blvd., Culver City, CA 90230; 310-397-8676
5945 Balboa Ave., San Diego, CA 92111; 858-565-9181
46 Geary Street, San Francisco, CA 94108; 415-781-5180

FLORIDA
145 S.W. 107th Ave., Miami, FL 33174; 305-559-6715

HAWAII
1143 Bishop Street, Honolulu, HI 96813; 808-521-2731
Neighbor Islands call: 800-259-8463

ILLINOIS
172 North Michigan Ave., Chicago, IL 60601; 312-346-4228

LOUISIANA
4403 Veterans Memorial Blvd., Metairie, LA 70006; 504-887-7631

MASSACHUSETTS
Rte. 1, 885 Providence Hwy., Dedham, MA 02026; 781-326-5385

MISSOURI
9804 Watson Rd., St. Louis, MO 63126; 314-965-3512

NEW JERSEY
561 U.S. Route 1, Wick Plaza, Edison, NJ 08817; 732-572-1200

NEW YORK
150 East 52nd Street, New York, NY 10022; 212-754-1110
78 Fort Place, Staten Island, NY 10301; 718-447-5071

OHIO
2105 Ontario Street, Cleveland, OH 44115; 216-621-9427

PENNSYLVANIA
9171-A Roosevelt Blvd., Philadelphia, PA 19114; 215-676-9494

SOUTH CAROLINA
243 King Street, Charleston, SC 29401; 843-577-0175

TENNESSEE
4811 Poplar Ave., Memphis, TN 38117; 901-761-2987

TEXAS
114 Main Plaza, San Antonio, TX 78205; 210-224-8101

VIRGINIA
1025 King Street, Alexandria, VA 22314; 703-549-3806

CANADA
3022 Dufferin Street, Toronto, Ontario, Canada M6B 3T5; 416-781-9131
1155 Yonge Street, Toronto, Ontario, Canada M4T 1W2; 416-934-3440

¡También somos su fuente para libros, videos y música en español!